Beneath the ICE

Faith, Fear, and the Disappearance of Justice in America

Jonah Ashcroft

SENTINEL RIDGE PUBLISHING
Atlanta, Georgia

Beneath the ICE:
Faith, Fear, and the Disappearance of Justice in America

© 2026 Jonah Ashcroft
All rights reserved.

No part of this book may be reproduced, stored in a retrieval system, or transmitted in any form or by any means—electronic, mechanical, photocopying, recording, or otherwise—without prior written permission of the publisher, except for brief quotations in reviews.

Published by Sentinel Ridge Publishing
Atlanta, Georgia

Printed in the United States of America

ISBN 979-8-9945691-0-8

Scripture quotations are taken from the *Holy Bible, English Standard Version® (ESV®)*.
Copyright © 2001 by Crossway, a publishing ministry of Good News Publishers.
Used by permission. All rights reserved.

This book is a work of nonfiction grounded in the author's lived experience. Certain names and identifying details have been altered to protect privacy and personal safety. Public officials, government personnel acting in their official capacities, and individuals whose conduct is a matter of public record or widely reported are identified by their real names. All accounts are presented in good faith and are based on firsthand knowledge, contemporaneous records, and publicly available information. Nothing in this work is intended to allege criminal conduct unless expressly stated as a matter of public record.

The author writes under a pseudonym Jonah Ashcroft to protect family members and others referenced in this work and reserves the right to disclose his identity should circumstances allow

Author's Note

This book is drawn from my own lived experience. The events, conversations, and encounters described herein are presented as I witnessed and understood them. I have made every effort to recount them truthfully and in good faith, while recognizing that they remain my perspective and interpretation of what occurred.

For reasons of personal safety and privacy, the author writes under a pseudonym. Some names have been omitted and others changed—often to biblical pseudonyms—while public officials, government personnel acting in their official capacities, and widely reported figures are identified by their real names.

Scripture quotations are taken from the English Standard Version (ESV) unless otherwise noted.

The author reserves the right to disclose his identity should circumstances allow.

*"Justice is turned back,
and righteousness stands far away;
for truth has stumbled in the public squares,
and uprightness cannot enter."*

—Isaiah 59:14 (ESV)

To the faithful brothers and sisters in Christ whose prayers and steadfast love carried us through seasons seen and unseen.

Contents

PART I

Into the Shadows: A Descent into America's Hidden System 1

PART II

Faith at a Price 49

PART III

America the Way It Is Not Supposed to Be 65

PART I

Into the Shadows: A Descent into America's Hidden System

PART I

Asher's Story

Asher sat on the hard, cold floor of an overcrowded detention room, thirty-five men pressed around him, the air thick and bitter, wondering if he would ever leave. He was sixty-three years old, a man with both Russian and Tajikistani passports. In March 2024, he was arrested and placed in removal proceedings. For the next eighteen months, he was moved from one detention center to another—first in California, then Texas, and finally Georgia, where he spent time in both the Folkston and Stewart County facilities. His final stop was the Central ICE Facility on Ted Turner Drive in Atlanta.

There, he spent eight days in an overcrowded room with roughly thirty-five other people. Days were suffocating. Nights were freezing. No showers were provided. No reasonable way to stay clean. On the seventh day, an ICE officer finally told him he was leaving. Asher cheered. The entire room cheered with him. At last, it seemed, he was going home. But the hours dragged on. No one came.

That Friday, he waited all day, clinging to hope, watching for his name to be called. Agents passed by. Voices echoed outside. Nothing happened. In the evening, another ICE officer showed him a phone with a Google translation into Russian: *"We are just waiting on a plane."* Asher laughed at the literal translation—"That doesn't make any sense." Long into the night, he held onto the promise. Finally, he fell asleep—broken-hearted.

The next morning, on Saturday—*sábado*, as I had been taught—after another crude breakfast, his name was finally spoken. He was told to gather his things. He was being deported at last. The room erupted in celebration—applause, stomping, shouting, banging on the plexiglass-like windows—joined by cheers from nearby cells. After eighteen months of detention, and eight grim, degrading days in Atlanta, Asher was finally leaving. He was going home.

The Larger Truth

This is one man's story, but it reveals a larger truth. America was not meant to be this way. It is a nation that proclaims liberty and justice for all, yet foreigners and strangers often encounter only cold walls, empty promises, and indifference. They stew in uncertainty, warehoused in crowded rooms, treated as less than human.

Americans still sing of freedom, but too often they look away from its absence. They speak of justice, yet tolerate systems that grind down the weak. They celebrate their exceptionalism, while stories like Asher's reveal a country deeply estranged from its own ideals.

Scripture commands, "Do not neglect to show hospitality to strangers, for thereby some have entertained angels unawares" (Hebrews 13:2). Yet America, a land so richly blessed, has drifted far from such a calling.

This is not the America it was supposed to be. And yet, to understand how it reached this place—and what it reveals about the soul of the nation—we must look more closely at the choices, stories, and illusions that have shaped it.

Wednesday - Part 1 - The Arrest

Five or six times a week, in the quiet of the morning, I walked at the local park across the street. Thirty minutes, roughly two thousand steps—a small rhythm that allowed me to pray, to lift before God the concerns of family, friends, and the wider world. This routine had become well established for me, but known only to two family members and a close friend.

On July 30, 2025, I followed my usual path, circling the top of a small hill overlooking the parking lot and returning toward the sidewalk that led out of the park. I was finishing my morning prayer when I noticed a Subaru creeping toward me as if about to leave the park. It paused, seemingly giving me the right of way, and I waved in thanks.

After I crossed and followed the path toward the exit, a sudden shout rang out behind me: "Sir!" I turned, expecting a jogger or hurried neighbor, but what I saw instead pierced the ordinary rhythm of the morning. In that moment, I glimpsed something that many Americans overlook: the quiet suffering, the frustration, and the loss of hope that often go unseen amid the nation's glitz, loud proclamations of success, and boisterous claims of promises kept.

At first, I saw a man who, at a glance, appeared to be a police officer. His vest bore the word *Police*, but there was no badge, no other identification—only a figure whose presence was heavily concealed. As I took in his full attire, it became clear that he was unlike any officer I had ever encountered. Tactical gear, heavy and intimidating, perhaps reminiscent of SWAT, covered him. His face was masked, his eyes hidden behind dark sunglasses, and a baseball cap shadowed his features.

Then he shouted, each word deliberate and punctuated by pauses: *"You . . . are under arrest . . . for the crime of being in this country illegally . . . on an expired visa."* In that instant, my mind struggled to reconcile what I had just been thinking with what I had just heard. Had I even finished my prayer and said *Amen*? A visa overstay is not a crime under the Immigration and Nationality Act (INA). Many immigration attorneys explain that it is a civil violation, the legal equivalent of a parking ticket. Yet,

PART I

as my thoughts raced, four more men appeared—similarly clad, broader, running and flanking me on both sides.

Commands followed—loud, harsh, insistent: *"Put your hands behind your back. I said, put your hands behind your back. Give me your phone."* Someone on my left forced my hand behind me, twisting my shoulder. My phone was taken, and my right hand was secured behind my back. In that moment, I understood: there would be no walking away. For whatever reason, these goons had been sent to take me.

When asked about health conditions, I mentioned my bad right knee and left shoulder. I was pushed against the SUV and handcuffed tightly. After a pat down, I was told to get in the back seat.

A Show of Force

As the three-vehicle convoy carried me and five of my captors away from the park, my mind raced: *Why me? Why now?* This was not a random or scheduled raid at a Home Depot, a construction site, or a "lucky" traffic stop. I had committed no crime, nor any act that would place me in the crosshairs of law enforcement. The last time I had pulled up my driving record—when I applied to take the Bar in California—it was blank.

I asked to see a warrant. My request was radioed to the man in charge, and I was told I would see it at the next stop.

The convoy itself felt deliberately intimidating and anonymous. None of the vehicles bore official markings. They were dark, heavily tinted. The one I rode in had police-type lights mounted inside, behind the back seat. Binoculars lay on the floor. The lead car, a Subaru, displayed a cheerful stick-figure family decal on the right and other decals on the left—an eerie juxtaposition against its dark windows. The vehicle behind was some kind of Toyota truck. It had stood out to me on at least two previous occasions, always parked in the same spot at the edge of the parking lot, its windows pitch-black—as if someone inside had been watching and waiting. What remained consistent across all three vehicles was the anonymity of the men: faces hidden, features erased, accountability concealed. This was not just an arrest; it was a show of force, a message.

As we passed my neighborhood, my heart sank. Would my parents and my brother find out that I was gone? Would my dog, Sherlock—my fifteen-pound Italian Greyhound—be okay in his crate? I remembered taking him out just before the walk—he had done his business outside and been crated. But how long would it be before anyone discovered that I was missing? How would my elderly parents—especially my father with his fragile health—process what had happened? And would anyone attempt to harass or intimidate them?

Into the Shadows

In that moment, I committed my fate to God, realizing that no matter what came next, He was in control. I prayed that He would protect my family and guide me on this unexpected journey.

Chains and Silence

Within minutes we pulled behind a Target, circling to the loading docks. The lot was empty. I was ordered out and told to face the vehicle. The men discussed whether to put me in full chains. Flanders, the man in charge, said yes.

He held up a document on his phone, calling it a warrant. I looked for a judge's signature—there was none. Instead, it was signed by his "boss." He dismissed my objections, saying, *"We will deal with all of that later."* My wrists were re-cuffed, now chained to a waist restraint, and my ankles were shackled. After I was ordered back into the vehicle, the group gathered and talked among themselves for several minutes. They were probably trying to get their story straight. Then we were off again. I asked where I was being taken and was told we were headed to the ICE facility in Atlanta for processing.

As we sat in morning traffic in front of Kohl's and PetSmart, my left shoulder throbbed sharply and the arm felt numb. Around me, the convoy's silence conveyed a message louder than words: authority could be exercised without accountability, and the human soul could be disregarded without pause, even for due process.

Scripture reminds us, "Learn to do good; seek justice, correct oppression; bring justice to the fatherless, plead the widow's cause" (Isaiah 1:17). Yet that morning, in the heart of a nation so richly blessed, justice seemed alien, and oppression deputized.

I prayed again as we drove. Earlier that morning, I had prayed for a higher calling and a people to serve. Now, bound and powerless, I prayed again—submitting to the journey God had placed before me. Submission brought peace, a peace that would sustain me in the days ahead.

Into the System

After more than an hour of driving—first down 141 and then onto 285—we arrived at a nondescript building hidden behind a fence topped with barbed wire. The driver swiped his card at the gate. One of the masked men opened the door. I understood then that it was time to step out.

The reception area was a gated overhang with two rows of plastic chairs facing each other. I was seated across from ten to fifteen men who appeared to be of Central or Latin American origin, and a few women placed farther down the row.

PART I

After some time, I was called forward to a table where an African American woman was placing people's belongings into large red bags that looked like oversized laundry sacks. I had brought only two items to the park that morning—my iPhone and my house key. The phone had already been confiscated and dropped into the bag. Flanders asked if I had anything else in my pockets, and I mentioned the key. Apparently the pat down had missed it. He pulled it out and handed it to the woman, who placed it in the bag as well, then told me to return to my seat and wait

We sat beside a spotless armored DHS vehicle, gleaming and seemingly unused. In this area, the differences among detainees were striking. Some wore standard cuffs, others only zip ties. One older man—Felix—was able to slip a hand free entirely. I alone remained chained with full restraints, as though I were waiting to board the infamous Con Air flight with Nicholas Cage.

The men bringing new detainees in all seemed cut from the same cloth. They were not law enforcement officers in the usual sense. They looked like contractors—former military, perhaps from another branch of law enforcement, deputized under ICE authority. Their appearance was unkempt, their uniforms nonexistent. The only thing marking them as state agents was a small badge clipped to the right hip. Clothing and firearms appeared to be a matter of personal choice. Some looked as though they may have dabbled in PEDs or other substances.

They resembled a ragtag team of former special operations soldiers, or those adjacent to that world, still grooming themselves as though preparing for another deployment to Afghanistan—beards and all. About half wore T-shirts branded with companies like Black Rifle Coffee, fully embracing the "vet-bro" lifestyle. To me, it seemed these men were reliving their "glory days," only now their mission was on American soil, and their targets were unarmed civilians. A few women who passed through the area were also armed, or else wore empty holsters on their waists.

Law enforcement officers are trained to understand, respect, and enforce the law, even though abuse still occurs despite that training. By contrast, ICE and its deputized "vet-bros" neither understand the law nor show respect for it. They are paid to carry out internal interpretations of the law, even when doing so violates constitutional protections.

After a time, an intake form was handed to me. I declined to fill it out. Even if I had wanted to, the chains made writing nearly impossible. I asked how much longer it would be before I could make a phone call. The response was curt: "After processing—three to four hours."

More detainees trickled in until every chair in the waiting area was filled. Some had to stand. Then Flanders returned and called me into a cramped processing office. The air was stale, the space confining. He asked me a few questions, which I refused to answer. He shrugged, almost relieved. "That's fine," he said. "Makes my job easier."

He explained that I could refuse almost everything except three things: a headshot, fingerprinting, and biometrics. Refusal, he warned, would only lead to force. Still chained, I was photographed. Fingerprinting proved a clumsy ordeal for everyone involved—the restraints made it awkward and nearly unworkable, and their machine was faulty.

Afterward, I was returned to my chair. Moments later, Flanders appeared again, suddenly remembering that my shoelaces had not yet been removed. He ordered me to take them out, then noticed the obvious: my restraints made it nearly impossible. "Oh, I totally forgot you still had those on," he muttered before disappearing again. He returned with a key, removed the chain around my waist, and directed me to lift my legs so he could free my ankles, though the handcuffs stayed on. I pulled the laces from my shoes and handed them over. Then it was back to waiting again.

Eventually, he returned and told me to follow him once more, this time through the same cramped processing room and into a secured area behind a keypad and a retina scanner. Beyond it lay what appeared to be an abandoned office section—no personnel, just cubicles used mostly for storage. From there, I was led into a conference room with a long table. Three more people followed—an overweight, balding man with glasses in his mid-fifties, and two women.

The Extra Extra "Interview"

The door shut with a heavy, deliberate thud. I was directed to sit at one end of the table. To my right sat the heavyset man, with Flanders across from me. The two women took seats to my left.

The young woman on my immediate left, white and restless, fidgeted with her hair and shifted repeatedly in her chair, as though searching for a position of control or comfort. The second, who appeared to be of Asian descent, carried herself with more restraint—her demeanor quiet, observant, and measured.

At that point, the man on my right began introductions. Gesturing toward Flanders across the table, he remarked, "You already met." He then identified himself.

"My name is John Cwieka. I am a Special Agent with the Department of Homeland Security. Your father may have mentioned me to you."

In that moment, everything—the events of the day and my father's prior encounters with this particular agent—began to align.

Initially, I thought this was a simple mistake—a bureaucratic overreach. But when I considered the amount of manpower committed to arresting me early in the morning at a small local park, I realized there was something else at play. As the hours passed and as Cwieka mentioned my father by name, it became clear this wasn't about me alone. It was about something that began long before me and far beyond me.

His tone confirmed that this was not random enforcement; there was an agenda. The questions had nothing to do with my presence in the United States. What they wanted from me was something else entirely. What I didn't yet grasp was that I had stepped into the same shadow that had followed my parents for years.

Cwieka wasn't bluffing. For years, federal agents had scrutinized and questioned my father over his ministry's ties to the Russian National Prayer Breakfast. They had turned a minister's calling into a national-security inquiry, twisting the language of faith into the vocabulary of suspicion.

That realization settled like a weight in the room. I understood then that this moment—this "interview"—was not a beginning but an echo, the repetition of a story written long before I ever sat at this table.

I responded to Cwieka, "Yes, you questioned him at the airport for four hours."

There was a prolonged pause. It was not the response Cwieka appeared to be seeking. I recalled my father's last encounter with him and another agent, likely from the FBI, at the airport. On that occasion, my father had been subjected to an extended interrogation, during which his electronic devices were confiscated.

Cwieka then introduced the two women as agents with the Federal Bureau of Investigation. Pointing first to the white woman, he said, "She is with the FBI." (Possibly: "She is an FBI agent.") Then, gesturing to the other, he added, "She is with the FBI too." (Possibly: "She is an agent too.")

At that moment, sitting across from Cwieka and the two FBI agents, I realized this was no ordinary detention interview. The pieces began to fall into place—everything was orchestrated, deliberate. And in the silence that followed, the questions I had tried to push aside—Why me? Why now?—revealed their answer.

Then came his first substantive statement. With a smirk, Cwieka leaned back in his chair slightly and said, "My position gives me the power to make this process much easier for you." (It is possible the exact phrasing was: "I have the power to make this process much easier for you.")

I either gave no response or simply replied, "Okay."

He continued. "The door to this room is closed. We are not recording this. No one can hear us. It is just the four of us and you—so you may speak freely."

Pause.

"We are interested in information on Russia."

Another pause.

"Specifically, Russian operations in the United States. We are not asking for general public knowledge—we want something that is not widely known."

At this, I may have raised my eyebrows. Being of Slavic descent, my face comes with subtitles.

I replied, "I would like to speak to my lawyer before I make any statements or discuss anything. And based on my lawyer's advice, I will proceed accordingly."

I understood, having completed my legal training and guided by extensive commentary from attorneys both online and in person, that in circumstances such as this, remaining silent was the prudent course. It offered little comfort that I was assured the conversation was not being recorded; government agents lie with ease and frequency, and Cwieka in particular had proven himself a profuse liar. His prior interactions with my father and others had already established him as fundamentally untruthful.

Even if there were no recording, any statements I made would be twisted or misrepresented by the four individuals present in the room—I was certain of that. I had seen it firsthand in the Notice of Intent to Revoke my father's Form I-360, and in the way they misrepresented and abused the statements of the senior pastor of the sponsoring organization and signatory of the petition.

Additionally, I realized they were not merely seeking information—they were searching for another Russian "operative" in the mold of Maria Butina. They needed someone to become the face of a new wave of Russian meddling in American affairs, someone to blame—hiding the failures of American diplomatic and political dealings with Russia on the international stage.

From my perspective, these actions were the result of an outdated mode of operation by these agencies and a complete failure to understand Russia.

If the FBI—or any similar agency—had wanted to arrest me, they would have been required to obtain a warrant signed by a judge, supported by probable cause. Without such a warrant or lawful exception, any arrest would have been unconstitutional. If I had been taken into custody and questioned, I would have been entitled to Miranda warnings. In my case, they had neither probable cause nor lawful basis—because there was no crime, no evidence— I was innocent.

By contrast, ICE has operated on a massive scale, systematically bypassing constitutional safeguards. These violations are not isolated incidents; they occur routinely, targeting countless individuals while the agency shields itself from accountability. ICE agents often conceal their identities, appearing in Antifa-style masks and unmarked vehicles, creating an atmosphere of intimidation and fear, all while disregarding the procedural protections guaranteed by the U.S. Constitution and the Bill of Rights.

To my relief—and their frustration—they had chosen the wrong person to extract information regarding Russian operations. My knowledge in that area was no greater than my understanding of nuclear fission or, humorously, the migratory habits of Canadian geese. Their line of inquiry was not only futile; it was crude and entirely misplaced.

There was a long silence. Then Cwieka responded, "You are certainly welcome to try and hire a lawyer. Or maybe your father can find one for you.

In fact, today or tomorrow I am going to stop by the house, because I have some documents to give your father."

I asked, "Why am I even here? I have no criminal record, and I have committed no crime."

My question referred to the fact that I had been arrested not by a single officer, but by five men—each overdressed for what was essentially an in-person service of a Notice to Appear, which could have been done by mail. For whatever reason, DHS and ICE decided that the best policy was to accomplish this via arrest and detention. However, such a display consumed enormous time and resources, all at taxpayer expense. Mail a letter, or send three vehicles with five men—which is better in terms of responsible spending?

After another prolonged silence, Cwieka replied, "I am aware that you have no criminal record, and that you have committed no crime. But the rules have changed."

I kept the comment—The rules may have changed, but the U.S. Constitution hasn't—to myself.

After a pause, I asked, "What's next?"

Cwieka responded, "You will be processed and detained for the duration of the removal proceedings."

I said, "Okay," and then asked, "Can I make a phone call?"

He replied, "That's fine." At that point, someone asked, "Do you have the numbers memorized?"

I answered, "No," explaining that while I roughly remembered one of my family member's phone numbers, I was uncertain whether I had it correct.

At this point, the female FBI agent sitting closest to me interjected, "No one has the phone numbers memorized anymore."

I was then handed my cellphone and instructed to pull up the numbers and dictate them. The FBI agent tore out a sheet of paper from her notepad and began writing as I dictated three phone numbers.

While doing so, I mentioned, "I have an appointment to get a haircut today—can I call and cancel?"

The group chuckled, and Cwieka remarked, "That is the least of your concerns right now."

I clarified, "So, can I call and cancel?"

He responded, "No."

Once the numbers were recorded, I was instructed to turn off my phone. Cwieka commented, "So it has a charge and you can use it when you get out."

I said, "Okay."

I was then told to stand. As we were heading out, Cwieka tried again. "You know, I will not be available to meet with you and your lawyer, if you do get one, to discuss anything"—making yet another attempt to pressure me to reconsider my refusal to provide "information."

I replied, "You are a tough man to get a hold of anyway," referring to the fact that my father and his attorneys had all tried, without success, for months to contact Cwieka in order to get information or retrieve my father's confiscated electronic devices.

In fact, more than a year later my father's iPhone was still not returned, a device that both Cwieka and whoever reviewed it admitted contained nothing unlawful.

Cwieka responded, "Well, you see how busy we are."

I later learned, from others in detention, that my "interview" was very unusual. Typically there was only the arresting or processing immigration officer present. In my case, however, there was a DHS special agent and two agents from the FBI.

ICE Field Office

We proceeded to what I believe was the operations center of ICE in Atlanta—a large room arranged with three rows of long stainless-steel counters, each equipped with five or six, perhaps more, operational computers and monitors. The furthest row contained large displays monitoring the cells, cameras, and overall facility operations. Along the right wall a large screen projected ongoing activities, and adjacent to it were two metal cabinets, one labeled *FUGOPS* and the other with a designation I cannot recall.

The operations center was surrounded by five or six holding cells. If my memory serves correctly, two, perhaps three, of the larger cells—Rooms 1 and 2—typically housed thirty or more people. The smaller cells, running perpendicular to the larger ones, appeared designated for medical segregation, women, and possibly other custodial purposes. Signs on each door stated in bold letters that "detainees" must remain in handcuffs at all times when outside their cells.

At the first row of tables, I was told I could make a phone call, though it had to be on speakerphone for a reason that seemed trivial. I dialed the first number—no answer. I tried the second—no answer. I tried the last—again, no answer. I was told I could try again later, after processing. I was uncertain what the DHS or FBI personnel expected me to say, or whom they anticipated I would contact.

After an awkward pause, the arresting agent escorted me past Holding Room 2, which appeared extremely crowded yet strangely animated, as if reacting to my presence. We proceeded to Holding Room 1, which was less crowded. The officer remarked, "I will put you in here, it is less crowded," then removed my handcuffs at the doorway and instructed, "Get inside."

I entered the room, which contained approximately seven to ten people, some of whom were sleeping. Room 1 mirrored Room 2—a room I would observe on multiple occasions during prolonged hours of boredom and sleeplessness as I sought to occupy my mind with something.

PART I

The room measured roughly twelve cinder blocks in width, nineteen in length, and thirteen in height. Like Edmond Dantès in *The Count of Monte Cristo*, I counted the cinder blocks, though I never reached the point of naming them. Given that a standard cinder block measures sixteen by eight inches, the space translated to about sixteen feet wide, twenty-five feet long, and eight feet, eight inches tall. Immediately upon entry, a short wall—five or six cinder blocks high—divided the space, with a stainless-steel bench on either side.

On the left, a stainless-steel bench ran approximately half the length of the room and terminated at another cinder block wall, which separated the main area from a stainless-steel fixture housing a toilet (without a seat) and a sink. A second cinder block wall divided this fixture from another stainless-steel toilet and sink. The two fixtures differed in design; one appeared to be constructed for handicap accessibility, though the reasoning for the variation was unclear.

On the right-hand side, a stainless-steel bench extended the full length of the room, ending at a short bench adjacent to the cinder block wall that separated the main room from the two toilet fixtures.

I found a spot on the bench along the left side, near the toilets, and attempted to make myself comfortable on the short mats, each about four feet long and eighteen to twenty inches wide. The mats were thin—perhaps three-quarters of an inch thick—but compressed dramatically under weight, reducing to little more than padding.

As I did not speak Spanish, and the others had limited English, communication was minimal. The only connection I managed was identifying myself as from Russia—*Rusia* in Spanish. One man offered me a small bottle of water, which I gratefully accepted, and a fruit cup containing mandarin slices in syrup, which I declined.

No one explained the specific designation of each toilet in the room. I did not understand at first, though I gradually pieced it together later. In Room 1, the furthest toilet from my bench was intended for solid waste, while the closest was for urination. By mistake, I used the furthest toilet for urination on two occasions, though I ensured that I cleaned the surface after each use out of consideration for others.

I spent what felt like several hours in this room—thinking, praying, and wondering about my family's well-being, about my dog, and hoping that my family would take the initiative to consult an immigration attorney. During this time, a man from Brazil was brought into the room. He introduced himself as Reuben, and later, we developed a friendship.

After several hours in Room 1, the arresting officer returned, placed me back in handcuffs, and escorted me to the first row of ICE operations counters—the same area where I had attempted a phone call earlier, though this time I was seated in a different spot. He presented a series of documents: a Notice to Appear, a Notice of Rights and Request for Disposition, a Notice of Custody Determination, a Warrant for Arrest of Alien, an Online Detainee Locator System printout, and a list of Pro Bono Legal Service Providers.

The officer reminded me that I could refuse to sign any of the documents presented, with the exception of one of the three mandatory requirements: biometrics. Refusal to comply with the biometrics would result in coercive enforcement and potential misdemeanor charges. I submitted to the procedure, which involved eight swabs applied to the inside of my cheeks.

Following the collection of biometrics, each of the documents was explained to me. I was told that I would be transferred to another ICE detention facility. When I asked for specifics, the officer responded that I would be sent to Stewart. When I inquired about its location, he stated that it was "on the border with Alabama—about two hours away." I then asked when the transfer would occur, and he replied, "today or tomorrow."

He further explained that because I had refused to sign any of the documents, I would automatically be assigned a bond hearing regarding potential release. When I asked how soon this would occur, he said two to three days. Reflecting on this later, it was unclear whether he was misinformed, misunderstood the procedure, or intentionally provided inaccurate information.

After the explanation of the documents, I was given another opportunity to make a phone call. The first number went unanswered, though I left a voicemail. The second went unanswered, without the option to leave a message. The third also went unanswered, though I again left a voicemail.

While I was on the phone, one of the ICE personnel—whose designation I could not confirm—contacted the arresting officer and requested that I be placed in Detention Room 2. Another Russian was present in that room, and because he did not speak English, I was asked to assist with translation. On the way to Room 2, I asked if I could be provided with a container for my contact lenses. The officer replied, "We don't have anything like that here."

Detention at ICE Room 2

I was not sure what to expect when entering a detention room—or cell. I had never been inside one before, except for a few occasions when I had visited Alcatraz on a tour. In my mind, I expected the people inside to be—well, more *criminal*. That was the image painted by the news media, echoing the claims of the current administration that they were pursuing "dangerous offenders" and "criminals" who were "invading" this country.

But when I stepped into Room 2, I was met with an entirely different reality.

The room was packed, crowded well beyond what seemed reasonable—there was scarcely enough space to stand. Yet despite the oppressive conditions, I received one of the warmest welcomes I can remember. As I entered, I was greeted with handshakes, hugs, and introductions.

Three individuals stood out immediately. Levi, from Zambia, carried himself with the strength and dignity of a warrior—as if fresh out of Wakanda. Mark, from Venezuela, extended kindness without hesitation. The third man—whose name I can no longer recall because I had no pen to write it down—helped to keep things organized and consistently looked out for me. The latter two, in particular, went out of their way to make me comfortable in that overcrowded room. They offered me water and found a mat to sleep on—something scarce in such conditions.

It took me some time to understand why everyone seemed genuinely happy to see me. The answer became clear when I was introduced to Asher. He was, in all likelihood, the oldest individual I encountered both at ICE and at Stewart. His English was extremely limited—no more than a handful of words—and he had been deteriorating mentally under the weight of waiting, compounded by the inability to communicate while surrounded by more than thirty other people. With my arrival, Asher finally had a friend he could talk to.

Once again, I was offered water—taken from someone's personal stash. One of the men explained the toilet arrangement: the first toilet was reserved exclusively for bowel movements (#2), while the one in the back was used for everything else—#1, brushing teeth, blowing noses, and any other task likely to cause splashing.

I sat down beside Asher, who had not spoken to his family in months and was desperate to communicate. We conversed for what felt like an hour, as he shared his story and his eighteen-month deportation ordeal. Time inside ICE detention seemed to lose all meaning, partly because of the utter unpredictability of the schedule and partly because, once I removed my dry contact lenses, I could no longer read the clock on the far wall.

Eventually, a late lunch was brought in—identical to breakfast and dinner. In some twisted sense, it could be described as "balanced."

The Meals

ICE served three meals a day: breakfast at approximately 6:00 a.m., lunch sometime between 11:00 a.m. and noon, and dinner after 6:00 p.m. My time estimates may be off because I could not read the clock. Each meal consisted of the same basic items, occasionally missing one or two components. The one constant was the burrito—beef and bean or cheese and bean—both apparently produced by El Monterey, "a family-owned company" based in Texas since 1964.

The burrito was accompanied by a small bag of chips (Cheetos, Lay's, or other brands heavy with artificial seasoning), one Oreo cookie—most often

Into the Shadows

Double Stuf, occasionally Golden—one, four-ounce Dole mandarin fruit cup, and a small Kirkland Signature bottled water, likely the eight-ounce size.

That Wednesday afternoon, I was not hungry. Prior to my detention, I had been following what I might call a "dirty" carnivore diet: six days a week, I ate a single evening meal of ground beef, cheddar cheese, eggs, preceded by several cups of coffee with cream throughout the day. Thursdays were my "cheat days." But more than dietary preference, the circumstances themselves suppressed any appetite I might have had.

I passed most of my food to Asher. He ate some immediately and saved the rest for later.

Conversations and Worship

Most of the men in the room spoke Spanish with only limited English. A few were conversational, but I spent most of my first hours talking with Asher. When he grew tired, he lay on a thin mat on the concrete floor, tucking his head beneath the stainless-steel bench in a futile attempt to escape the fluorescent lights that never dimmed.

As he rested, I observed my surroundings. Room 2 was a mirror image of Room 1, where I had been held earlier. The symmetry gave me a strange sense of orientation, but my greatest comfort came not from the architecture but from what I witnessed.

To the left of the entrance, a group had formed—men lying, sitting, and standing, all listening to a single speaker. This man, Felix, a fifty-five-year-old from Guatemala, spoke passionately for hours. Though I could not understand everything he said, I heard the Spanish names he repeated again and again: *Jesús* and *Dios*. He was preaching.

In the back corner, another conversation centered on Jesus—this one in English. Drawn by both language and subject, I joined.

This group included the three men who had caught my attention upon entering the room. Their kindness and respect transformed an otherwise unbearable experience into something more endurable.

Levi, was a Muslim from Zambia who had once served as a bodyguard for two of the country's presidents. He came to US on a visa and applied for asylum. His asylum application was neither granted nor denied, but he was issued a work authorization. At the time of his arrest by ICE, Levi was working at a car dealership, when five to six ICE agents showed up and detained him while he was on a phone call at work. He was fully chained, just like me, and marched out like a criminal in front of his colleagues and customers. He was brought into Room 2 while wearing his work clothes - dress slacks and shoes, and a dealership branded short-sleeved shirt.

Despite our differences in faith, we spent two hours discussing the Person of Jesus. There were points of disagreement, but the conversation remained warm and respectful. At one point, we even requested a Bible from an ICE agent, only to be told that none would be provided because someone had once tried to conceal an object inside one. We continued without a Bible, hopeful that we might reconnect after transfer and continue the discussion with Scripture in hand.

In that stark room, more than half the men were talking about Jesus. To me, it was a quiet reassurance that God was present with me—even there.

Physical Exertion and Hygiene

After a while, more men were brought into the room. One of them, also from Zambia, immediately connected with Levi. Soon after, partly from boredom and partly from excitement, a few of the men began doing push-ups to pass the time. I joined them. There was little else to do, and exercise offered a much-needed release from stress.

Not long after, another man arrived—Daniel, from Ghana. He had been picked up at his workplace, a bakery in Suwanee, and quickly joined our workout group. For a brief moment, the exercise gave us a sense of camaraderie and normalcy. When we finished, we cleaned ourselves as best we could with hygienic wipes that one of the men had persuaded the guards to provide. It would be the last time I—or anyone else—had access to such basic hygiene until the day of my transfer.

Dinner followed, identical to lunch: a burrito, a bag of chips, an Oreo, a fruit cup, and a bottle of water. I kept the water and the burrito—beef and beans that day—thinking this was as close to carnivore as I was likely to get. I gave the rest to Asher. Eating that burrito proved to be a mistake.

The Phone Call

Not long after dinner, my name was called by a member of the staff. This officer was one of the few at ICE who showed some measure of consideration. Known for occasionally giving out two bottles of water instead of one, he informed me that I would be permitted to make a phone call.

Handcuffed, I was led to the phone and given five minutes. To my relief, the call went through. I was able to speak with my family, update them on the day's events, and provide them with my A-number—the "detention Social Security number," as it was commonly called.

Knowing that I had reached them, that they were safe, and that Sherlock (our dog) was safe—though he had not eaten all day, sitting by the front window waiting—gave me a measure of reassurance. For a moment, it reminded me that things were not as dire as they might have seemed.

The brevity of that call left a deep impression on me. It reminded me to treasure every moment I have to speak with those I love and continues to serve as a lasting call to be intentional about how I use the time entrusted to me.

The Night in Room 2

The lights in these rooms are never turned off or dimmed. Fortunately, of the eight ceiling lights in our room, only two were on. As night approached, Mark warned me that sleep would be a challenge.

I had estimated that the benches lining the perimeter, along with the two short benches flanking the five-block-high wall near the entrance, could accommodate perhaps eleven men at most. Yet there were roughly thirty-five detainees. Periodically, a staff member would enter to conduct a headcount, recording the number on the small whiteboard affixed to the door.

Mark indicated the short bench as my sleeping spot, while he lay beneath it. The rest of the men arranged themselves wherever possible—some on benches, most on the floor—pressing the four-foot mats against the cold concrete for minimal comfort. Sleeping on the floor had one small advantage: one could tuck a head beneath a bench to shield oneself from the harsh overhead light.

I was warned that the nights could grow cold—a detail I had not fully considered. Earlier that day, the room had felt warm, nearly stifling during exercise, but as the night wore on, the chill set in.

There were only five or six thermal blankets—thin, reflective, foil-like sheets that rustled loudly at every movement. Neither mats nor blankets were sufficient for everyone. When we requested more, we were told none were available.

The Smell of Confinement

I was reminded of my first visit to the Fulton County Animal Shelter, when I nearly adopted a one-year-old boxer. Walking into that shelter, I was struck first by the smell, then by the sight of terrified, unwashed dogs in a space too small for them.

The ICE rooms had no waste on the floor, but the odor was similar—not from animals, but from human bodies. Detainees had been confined for days or weeks, some after spending time in jail, and even those from non-labor jobs developed a noticeable scent within a single day.

This was one more reason I avoided the artificially flavored snacks. Our bodies excrete what we consume, and I did not want to add to the already oppressive smell in the room.

PART I

Sleeping Arrangements and the Loss of Privacy

Those who slept on the floor were packed shoulder to shoulder, hip to hip—like sardines in a can. Some detainees who had been there longer shared a single thermal blanket, which could barely cover three people if they lay tightly together.

The lack of privacy was perhaps the most difficult aspect for many. Men shielded their faces with an arm, a shirt, or anything that could block the sight of a stranger's head inches from their own.

The clothing of many bore traces of hard labor—mud, dust, and grime tracked across the floor until it settled on every surface. Any thought of cleanliness became impossible. Germs, smells, and dirt were simply part of existence.

A Night Without Rest

By contrast, I was fortunate to have my own relatively private sleeping spot. I did not have to feel another human's breath on my face or neck, nor did I have to breathe onto another person. Having my own bench was an advantage for a somewhat restless sleeper like myself, as I could roll from side to side without disturbing anyone.

I typically pray twice a day at set times—once in the morning during my walk and once at night, offering thanks for the events of the day. On my first night at ICE, despite the circumstances, I followed this routine. I offered thanks for the day that had passed, trusting that God had a plan, even in a situation so far beyond my control. My prayer included a plea for protection —for God to watch over my family, shield me from illness, and guard me against malicious individuals I might encounter. Looking back, I do not believe I met a single person with harmful intent toward me. It was as though the Lord's hand guided and protected me, quietly and unseen, throughout that first night and in the days that followed.

I did not sleep at all. The room did not quiet down until midnight, perhaps later. Conversations were the primary means of passing time, and with little else to do, they continued well into the night. Eventually, the chatter subsided, but the collective noise—the unimaginable variety of snoring, shifting bodies, the deafening flush of toilets, and the constant hum and glare of fluorescent lights—made rest impossible.

Shortly after midnight, my stomach reminded me that the burrito had been a mistake. I began to consider how to manage gastrointestinal discomfort over the coming days. Then, around 1:00 a.m., I understood why the nights grew so cold: the air conditioning, dormant during the day, roared to life and stayed on until five or six in the morning.

Though I had a bench to myself, the HVAC vents were positioned directly over the two short benches near the front of the room. That first night

I was shivering and uncomfortable, rolling from side to side in search of relief. I had yet to discover how best to use the flimsy four-foot mat. Later I learned to fold it as a pillow—my standard approach as my body adjusted to the steel surface of the bench.

The Morning Routine

Thursday morning began with the clang of the cell door and the delivery of "breakfast." Among the detainees, every meal was called *burrito*—a term understood by both English and Spanish speakers. I already despised the sight of them and gave my meal to Asher, keeping only the bottled water.

But I still had to deal with the burrito I had eaten the night before. Normally, a thermal blanket—or a scrap of one—served as a privacy curtain for the stall reserved for #2. That morning, however, all blankets were in use by those still sleeping, as the room remained bitterly cold. I communicated my need to Mark—"el baño," I said—and he nodded with understanding. Without hesitation, he retrieved a blanket from a sleeping man. Together with the detainee who had first greeted me, Mark arranged mats, the blanket, and water bottles to provide as much privacy as possible.

Two men I had just met were making sure I could go in comfort.

The odors were unavoidable, but the solution was simple: flush as you go. The industrial flushers were so powerful that they pulled even some of the air down with them. Those who forgot this step were quickly reminded by the room with shouts of, "Push the button!" or "¡Púshalo!" Once again, strangers were helping me in a moment of need.

We were all bound by circumstance—kidnapped, removed, or torn from our lives and deposited into a reality defined by uncertainty and helplessness. I was grateful for the relief and resolved to fast until dinner on Friday. Fasting had become familiar to me over the past several years, and I had no difficulty subsisting on coffee alone for forty-eight to seventy-two hours. Though I had failed many times to quit coffee—missing the taste, the aroma, and suffering headaches—on Wednesday I experienced none of those symptoms. Thursday morning brought no headache either—a small but unmistakable reminder of God's grace in the midst of my confinement.

Prayer as Anchor

As the morning went on, I reminded myself that I needed to establish rhythms to keep my spirit lifted and my mind steady. I returned to my habit of prayer, as though I were on my morning walk in the park. My petitions carried a sharper edge now—I prayed not only in gratitude but also for protection, peace, and hope.

Morning and evening prayer became my two anchors, sustaining me spiritually and emotionally. Each prayer was a deliberate reaching toward God, an act of surrender to the One who holds all things in His hands. It was a way to give thanks in every circumstance and to remember that nothing—not confinement or uncertainty—could separate me from His presence or His plan.

Losses and Small Graces

My eyes ached from lack of sleep, and I still had my contacts in with nowhere to store them. I tried rinsing them with bottled water and somehow managed, without a mirror, to put them back in. They dried out again almost immediately. Hoping to salvage them, I dropped them into a small water bottle, imagining they might rehydrate. It was futile.

Several times I tried to put them back in, with other detainees offering bottled water and warning me not to use the tap water. Without a mirror, the effort was impossible. Eventually, the contacts were mistaken for trash and thrown away—another small loss in a place where comforts were constantly stripped away.

Cleanliness was nothing more than a dream. The wipes we had received the day before were gone, leaving only a bottle of pink hand soap and a bottle of Purell sanitizer. I resorted to applying Purell to toilet paper and scrubbing my exposed skin. The chemicals burned and caused peeling, but at least I felt briefly cleaner.

Later that afternoon, a broom and dustpan were brought in, and we were given three minutes to sweep. With more than thirty men in the room, mats and bodies could be shifted quickly. Then came a bucket and mop—though the bucket was empty. Ingenuity took over: empty water bottles were filled at the tap and poured into the bucket, with soap and sanitizer mixed in to make a crude cleaning solution. The men cleaned systematically—sleeping areas first, toilets last. It made sense.

Yet the effort proved fleeting. The room was far beyond capacity, and with every new arrival came more dirt, debris, and the grime of restless bodies pressed together. Within minutes, the room was filthy again.

Growing Resignation

That day I did not get to speak with my family. Only later did I learn the rule: detainees were guaranteed just two phone calls—one after processing, another before transfer. In between, there was only silence.

I fell asleep in an awkward position after dinner, exhausted from the past two days and sleepless night. But sometime before midnight, I awoke as if from a nightmare. For a moment, disoriented, I struggled to remember where

I was. When I realized it was not a dream—and that this reality was not going away—I did the only thing I could: I prayed—for help, for sanity, for protection, and for my family.

Sleep remained elusive. Though I folded my mat as a pillow, I lay awake through most of the night. When Friday morning arrived, I was physically drained. Yet despite the lack of rest, I noticed a shift within me. My stomach, finally empty, had settled. My body was weary, but my spirit was at peace. Through the long hours of darkness, I had called out to God again and again, and He had answered with quiet strength.

Conditions remained wretched—the stench, the filth, even my own body now joining the odor of the room. But I had come to terms with where I was. I had not been transferred to Stewart on Wednesday or Thursday, as Flanders had promised. Nor had I received any notice of an "automatic" bond hearing. After returning home, I learned that these automatic bond hearings were automatically denied.

Still, I found myself fully surrendered to God. He was in control, and I was simply along for the ride.

Friday and the Hallucinations

Staying awake through the night, I prayed my morning prayer early. It was something concrete, something reliable, that I could cling to amid the uncertainty and the wandering of my mind.

That Friday morning I gave my burrito breakfast to Asher, who gratefully accepted it. Later we heard that he was scheduled to be deported, and everyone celebrated with him. But when the transfers began, his name was never called.

Levi, Mark, and the third man from their trio were all transferred. We said our goodbyes, wishing each other well and holding onto the faint hope that we might meet again at Stewart. Soon after, the second Zambian man and Daniel from Ghana were also moved. I never saw them again.

By evening, when the next "burrito" arrived, I could no longer stomach the sight of one. The mandarin fruit cup became my only food. Normally I avoid fruit and sugar except on Thursdays, but I poured out the syrup and ate the mandarin slices.

Because I kept giving most of my meal away, Asher, Felix, and others began giving me their fruit cups. Soon even men I had not spoken to—men with whom I shared no common language—were freely handing me theirs. These so-called "criminals" gave without hesitation.

Friday night came, and Asher, broken-hearted, drifted into sleep, his hoped-for deportation postponed again. After praying, I too tried to rest, but sleep would not come. I had heard that after several nights without sleep, the mind begins to hallucinate.

PART I

To my amazement, as I stared into the unlit light fixtures above me, visions appeared—Bedouins on camels crossing deserts, ships cutting through seas, and armies of horsemen galloping with swords drawn. The images were so vivid that several times I stood up to check whether some hidden screen had been placed in the lights, visible only to me. That is how real it was.

Prepared for the Trial

Between failed attempts to sleep and the strange spectacle above my head, I prayed—simple, childlike prayers—calling out to God again and again for help. In that place of exhaustion and weakness, peace returned to me.

That night I realized that, in a way, I had been prepared for this moment. Spiritually, I was in the right place. Not long before, I had finished reading Charles Swindoll's *Insights on Philippians, Colossians, and Philemon,* where he reflects on Paul and Silas in prison—beaten, confined, with every reason to be bitter and angry at their captors, yet responding with joy and trust in God. I had also completed the book of Daniel and its commentary, with its accounts of faithful men who faced trials but never abandoned their trust in the Lord.

Most of all, I had been meditating on Philippians 4:13: "I can do all things through Him who strengthens me." That verse is so often taken out of context as a motivational slogan for dreams or ambitions, but its true meaning speaks of contentment in every circumstance—especially the hard ones. As Paul writes,

"I know how to be brought low, and I know how to abound. In any and every circumstance, I have learned the secret of facing plenty and hunger, abundance and need" (Philippians 4:12).

Paul's secret was reliance on Christ's strength. With Him, all things are possible—and Paul was right.

For several years, my focus had been learning contentment. In detention, I found it. Because I had been prepared spiritually, I was able to remain steady emotionally. Though frustration came with the uncertainty and the lack of information, my spirit stayed lifted. Physically, I was also in a good place. My carnivore diet—eliminating sugar and carbs except for my Thursday "cheat day"—kept me calmer and more balanced, free from insulin spikes or energy crashes, and my body felt healthy and strong. Fasting was not difficult. Together, my spiritual and physical preparation allowed me to endure this trial with peace and a positive mindset.

Felix's Friendship

After Asher was finally deported on Saturday, I formed a deeper friendship with Felix. He was the kind of man who seemed to have made it his mission to speak with every Spanish-speaking person about Jesus—sometimes for hours. To my amazement, people listened.

Felix told me about his wife and two children: a son skilled with his hands and a daughter still in high school who played the violin. His troubles began one day while walking his dog, a pit mix named Canelo—after the boxer. A neighbor, who disliked the breed, called the police. When officers arrived, they told Felix to tie Canelo to a tree and call his family to pick the dog up. Soon afterward, Felix was taken to jail and later transferred to ICE detention.

Felix looked out for me in ways I did not expect. He and I were the only ones who spoke conversational English; the rest spoke only Spanish. He always made sure I had a place in line for the rare, precious phone calls to family—even offering me his spot once, which I declined.

Once again, I was struck by the kindness of strangers. These were men who, at first glance, looked dirty and disheveled—who smelled, as we all did by that point—but beneath the grime were hearts full of generosity and thoughtfulness.

The Toll of Confinement

By Saturday, the lack of showers and constant contact with filthy surfaces began to take its toll. My skin, already raw from scrubbing with Purell on toilet paper, now burned with every touch against my shorts or another surface. Pink and red spots began appearing—suspicious, stubborn, and concerning.

By God's grace, I had worn a T-shirt from Perimeter Church's Men's Retreat. Its ultra-soft fabric resisted odors and did not irritate my skin, a small mercy amid the filth. But my other clothing, unwashed and grimy, worsened the irritation. Despite my efforts at cleanliness, the condition lingered. I worried not only for my health but also about infecting my cellmates—or contracting something from them.

Just before lunch, one of the staff members stopped to count the detainees. There were nineteen men in the room—the lowest number we had seen—yet he mistakenly wrote sixteen on the whiteboard. Only sixteen burritos were prepared. When we pointed out the error, the staffer grew angry, slammed the door, and blamed us. Because I was mostly fasting, I gave my food away, and others shared what little they had.

Later more people were brought in, including another man from Zambia—fifty-two years old but looking no older than forty. He had been arrested because the ankle monitor ICE had given him malfunctioned, prompting ICE to show up at his home to re-detain him.

That evening, I resolved to eat only two mandarin fruit cups a day, hoping that limiting sugar and fuel might slow the spread of whatever infection I was fighting. Sleep came in fragments—an hour at a time—interrupted by strange visions, whispered prayers, and shivering once the air conditioning roared on. Yet even in exhaustion and discomfort, my spirits remained surprisingly high.

Silence and Waiting

By Sunday I kept to the same sparse diet. Seeing my restraint, the men began giving me their fruit cups, though I still limited myself to two per meal, letting the rest accumulate into a small stash.

The burning in my skin worsened, and I decided that after Sunday dinner I would fast completely for at least a day, starving whatever sickness might be trying to take root.

On Monday—the sixth day of my detention—we were told to take our mats outside for cleaning. We were gathered by in the waiting area with the large DHS truck. Each of us was given a few hygienic wipes—one set for the mats and another for our bodies—as well as toothbrushes. I saved two wipes to use later in the cell, determined to clean myself more thoroughly and privately.

As the only white man in the room, I always stood out. One ICE agent seemed surprised I was still there, a reaction that deepened my suspicion that my prolonged detention was deliberate—a tactic to stall, delay, and deny me access to legal remedies. And to make my family's circumstances more unbearable—to put them in a bad spot.

My family had already contacted an attorney, and I held onto the faint, cinematic hope that he or she might burst through the doors, Harvey Specter–style, demanding my release on grounds of unlawful arrest. But that moment never came—and in truth, it was never likely to.

The hard reality is this: when a person is first taken into ICE custody, communication is severely restricted. Attorneys often struggle to locate their clients, calls go unanswered, and detainees have little to no ability to reach legal counsel. During this "processing" period, days or even weeks can pass before any meaningful legal action can be taken.

Bond hearings or custody redeterminations are not automatic, and for many detainees, requests are delayed or denied outright. Judges may be constrained by administrative priorities and limited authority, leaving detainees effectively without recourse. Until a transfer is completed to a long-term detention facility such as Stewart or Folkston, even filing a basic Motion for a Bond Redetermination Hearing can be nearly impossible.

The result is a procedural limbo in which due process is functionally suspended. Every hour spent in this legal gray zone heightens the sense of powerlessness — shutting doors to legal protection and keeping families, attorneys, and detainees themselves in the dark.

Attorneys who try to intervene quickly learn the futility of it. Calls, filings and judge's orders are ignored or brushed aside with the same well-worn excuses: "We're too busy" or "We're waiting for this or that." These phrases have been repeated for so long that they no longer even pretend to carry legitimacy. This is not busyness; it is entrenched dysfunction. It is not delay; it is systemic neglect and incompetence weaponized into abuse.

And it works. It breaks many people. It kills hope, drains resolve, and wears down the spirit until detainees resign themselves to a system designed to uproot them from their lives, separate them from their families, and discard them without due process.

Transfer to Stewart

On Monday evening I was told I would be transferred to Stewart. Before leaving, I was allowed a brief call to my family to tell them. In the staging area, I saw Reuben again—he too was being moved that night.

The ordeal of preparing for transfer was exhausting. Each detainee was placed in full restraints, a process that dragged on for hours. The officers tasked with securing us moved with agonizing slowness—so obese that every movement left them gasping for air and drenched in sweat—making the entire ordeal even longer.

By the time the process was finished, the transfer that had begun around 8:00 p.m. did not have us on the bus until nearly 11:00.

I managed to sit next to Reuben, one of the last available seats. Three women—likely from China—were placed in a separate section of the bus.

The ride felt like something out of a horror film or a dystopian novel. The bus became a kind of rocket propelled into a void. Darkness pressed against the windows, broken only by the occasional flash of headlights. The hard seats amplified every bump and jolt of the road, while the absence of clocks stripped away all sense of time.

It felt less like travel and more like surrender—an unmarked descent into the unknown, heavy with foreboding, as though time and space themselves had been taken away.

Detention at Stewart

Stewart Detention Center, located in Lumpkin, Stewart County, Georgia, is a privately operated prison run by CoreCivic (NYSE: CXW) under contract with U.S. Immigration and Customs Enforcement (ICE). The facility is officially designed to hold 1,752 detainees, but during my time there the intake board consistently showed numbers well above that threshold. On three separate occasions I recall seeing counts between 2,040 and 2,141—evidence that the facility was operating significantly over capacity.

Though privately owned, Stewart functions as part of the federal immigration system and serves as one of the main sources of employment for the small town of Lumpkin. Many residents work at the prison, making the detention center both the economic backbone of the community and a symbol of how immigration enforcement has been outsourced to profit-driven corporations.

We arrived well after 1:00 a.m. Once the chains were removed, we were divided into groups and corralled into small, freezing holding cells in Medical, still in our street clothes. Each room held about twenty people. Over the next few hours, we were given a perfunctory physical—blood pressure, heart rate, oxygen level, height, weight, and a few quick questions about chronic conditions and allergies. I weighed in at 180 pounds clothed—my lowest in decades. To my surprise, I measured five foot ten; I had "grown" two inches—the only positive note of the day—and my blood pressure was normal.

Intake: Cold, Delay, Disarray

After the quick exam, we were issued colored bracelets and left waiting in the icy room again. It felt less like a clinic waiting room and more like a gas chamber—concrete walls, tiled floors, and an AC vent blasting directly into the center. Hours later we were ordered to intake and issued our uniforms. The disorganized physicals had been my first glimpse into how Stewart was run; intake became my second. Despite the "processing" at ICE, the long bus ride, and the additional three hours in Medical, the staff were unprepared. They scrambled to find and label small blue bags for our street clothes, then handed out uniforms, the color determined by our bracelets.

At Stewart, uniforms came in four colors, each marking a different custody level. Blue and beige (or tan) signified low custody; some said blue was the very lowest. I was issued beige—though I still do not know the logic behind the choice. Orange marked medium custody, while red was reserved for high custody—those requiring individual escorts in the hallways. I later learned that red typically indicated a history of violent crime. From what I witnessed on the bus and during intake, only a small minority fell into that category—perhaps one in twenty.

Those in orange or red were kept separate from us. I crossed paths with the "reds" only three times: once while waiting for a video call with my lawyer, another time when ICE was trying to talk detainees into "voluntary departure," and finally just before my bond hearing.

After receiving three sets of uniforms (tops and bottoms), four sets of underwear, Victory Supply canvas shoes, rubber clogs, and a laundry bag filled with bedding and basic items, we were herded into a large room at the corner of the intake area. This was where the blue and beige groups would spend the next twelve hours or so.

Ordinarily the confinement might have been bearable, as many of us had already become accustomed to sleeping on concrete floors or tiled benches. But here, the HVAC system was broken. For half a day, we sat in a room that felt like a meat freezer. The blankets we were issued were thin and nearly transparent; wrapped around us, they did little to cut the chill. Sleep was impossible. There were no mats—only a hard concrete floor and a tiled surface running along the perimeter. A few curled up there, but most gave up; the cold seeped through everything. I am convinced nearly everyone caught a cold in that room.

Passing the Time

To pass the time, some turned to the only entertainment available: a language game. Someone would say a word or phrase, and others would translate it into their own tongue. As usual, Reuben was the ringleader, sparking laughter and distraction in a place otherwise defined by discomfort and waiting.

Reuben was from Brazil. He had come to the United States on a visa, married an American woman, and was a father to his American daughter, who turns three this September. He was in the middle of applying for a green card when ICE picked him up—ironically, on his way to court to deal with paperwork. Now he was in removal proceedings, his life and family suddenly hanging in the balance. At Stewart, he quickly became a friend. He often started the language game—"How do you say this in your language?" Simple, but it broke the silence and turned strangers into companions.

That is how I met a young man from Palestine, only twenty-three, detained with his older brother. Like Reuben, they had entered on visas. Both had applied for asylum—a claim that should be among the most compelling of our time. Yet because of the way DHS, ICE, and USCIS operate—with incompetence, indifference, and neglect—their cases languished. They received work permits but remained technically "deportable." That thin line of bureaucratic absurdity was all ICE needed to detain them and place them in removal proceedings.

The brothers were arrested; their homes, cars, and businesses searched; their phones seized and combed through. They were first taken to a local jail in South Carolina (as best I recall), where conditions were degrading to the point of cruelty. They slept on bare concrete floors without mats or blankets, using shoes as pillows, while guards kicked their meals under the door as if feeding animals. After days of that, they ended up on the same bus that brought me to Stewart.

PART I

The staff who arrived Tuesday morning seemed unconcerned about the freezing temperature. Their lack of surprise made it clear that malfunctioning systems were part of daily life at Stewart. Many things in the facility were broken. We could have spent far less time in that holding room had intake been efficient; instead, long stretches passed while staff chatted among themselves.

Housing: Blocks, Pods, and "Boats"

By Tuesday afternoon we were told to get up—time to go to our assigned pod. I later learned that Stewart had seven blocks. Blocks 1 through 3 housed the blue and beige uniforms, as far as I could tell. Each block had six pods, designed for forty bunks each. At any given time there were also at least ten "boats" in each pod. A "boat" was a plastic platform, about ten inches off the floor—made of the same molded material as a kayak—meant to hold a mattress. Sometimes these were placed in open spaces; sometimes they were jammed alongside bunks. Cramped and short on privacy, yes—but after sleeping on concrete and next to strangers in prior facilities, the arrangement felt almost tolerable.

I do not know the exact layout of Blocks 4 through 6, though I assume they were similar and housed women as well as higher-custody detainees in orange and red. Block 7A was designated for segregation, while 7B served as medical segregation.

New arrivals to a pod were always assigned a boat. I was placed in Block 2, Pod C. Since no boats were set up, we were told to retrieve them from storage. An older man named Rufus volunteered to help me. It took two people to carry a boat and another to carry a mattress. Rufus then showed me how to tie the ends of the sheet and pull it over the mattress—a fitted-sheet workaround.

Small Mercies: Meals, Showers, Yard

Once settled, we were told that lunch had been delivered. One of the few positives at Stewart was consistency: while the food was bad—very bad—it arrived three times a day. Sometimes extra portions were available for those working trash, cafeteria, or laundry detail. After a late lunch, I met José, who would come to my aid on many occasions and showed me kindness.

Another small relief: showers were generally available when not in use. I recall four standard shower stalls and one handicapped stall. The toilet stalls mirrored this layout: four standard and one handicapped. José immediately explained the system: the first two stalls were for #1, the last two for #2. I had already guessed as much—two of the stalls had curtains.

Finally, I did something I had eagerly anticipated for nearly a week—I took a shower. The immediate problem was that, sleeping on a boat instead of a bunk, I had no designated place to dry my towel. I draped it over the wall separating the main room from the showers and toilets. At first, I worried someone might take it; in hindsight, that concern was unnecessary.

Later that afternoon, we were called to the yard—"¡yarda! ¡yarda!" The yard was divided into sections: some had only a basketball or volleyball court; others included a soccer field; a few had pull-up bars. On my first day at Stewart, Reuben and I walked laps around the perimeter and talked.

Much of the time at Stewart was spent sitting around or trying to sleep. There were very few books, virtually no access to the so-called library, and I still did not have a Bible. What struck me immediately, however, was the generosity of those around me. People offered food, snacks, or assistance without hesitation. Having endured the struggle of being a fresh transfer, they understood the challenges.

The local food was unappealing, and many relied on items from the commissary. Generously, they always offered to share. I declined, believing it best to maintain a carnivore or keto regimen and eliminate unnecessary snacking. Eating only one meal a day, however, was impossible given the quality and quantity of food served at Stewart.

That night, the room stayed noisy until well after midnight, and the lights were dimmed late. Despite everything, I slept fairly well. The cold from intake had not yet become a serious issue, and for the first time in days, I felt a small measure of relief.

Wednesday: "Chow, comida"

On Wednesday—the second day at Stewart—around 6:00 a.m., the lights snapped on, followed by the soon-familiar shout: "Chow, comida! Chow, comida!" This was the call to breakfast, and every other meal. After the call, there was typically a wait of thirty minutes to an hour before we were let out. There was no schedule, no apparent plan—everything seemed random.

Breakfast was always the worst meal: strange baked biscuits, often watered-down grits, sometimes oatmeal—generally useless carbs—and, on two occasions, an apple. The "coffee" was faintly brown and most certainly not coffee. I gave away whatever I did not eat, and people were grateful.

A bright spot that morning was running into Levi and Mark in the cafeteria; they greeted me with hugs and smiles. After breakfast, I tried to sleep, but soon felt a tap on my foot. It was José with a pack of instant oatmeal, a pack of ramen, and an apple. We spoke briefly and shared our stories. I mentioned that I hoped to write down my experiences but had no pen—José immediately gave me one. I spent the next several hours recording everything that had happened since the previous Wednesday.

PART I

I also wrote my initials on the corners of my towels, worried someone might take them. It proved unnecessary. These so-called "criminals" and "illegals" did not steal.

A few days later, after I moved to a top bunk, I was drying two small towels on the rail. One fell during the night; in the morning, only one remained. I worried it was gone. While searching for my toothbrush, I opened my "locker"—the blue vinyl bag I had been issued—and found the missing towel inside. Apparently, when it fell, my neighbor below (or someone else) put it in my bag. There was no stealing. There was no fighting. In the first week, I saw only two arguments, both resolved calmly: one about a place in line for the microwave, and another over a tablet.

Cleanliness and Quiet Generosity

What surprised me daily was how carefully men kept themselves. Those whom many Americans might carelessly label "dirty Mexicans" brushed their teeth three to five times a day. Showers were extended events, and men stayed clean and well groomed. Even those with little to spare were generous, offering what they had to new arrivals.

Reuben developed a cough on the first or second day at Stewart. When he could not sleep in the middle of the night, someone offered him medicine; it worked almost immediately and eased his suffering.

Worship in the Pod

After lunch, around 1:00 p.m., our pod held the daily worship service for Spanish speakers. Like most pods, ours was roughly 85 percent Spanish speakers, with maybe 5 percent conversational in English. I experienced this service just after our arrival on my first day, and it felt exciting simply because it was new. Though I understood only a few words, it reminded me that God's presence remained—even here.

Yard Time and Burpees

Later that afternoon we were called to the yard. I was hopeful I would not spend much longer at Stewart, telling myself that a bond hearing would come soon, that the judge might grant it—or even release me on my own recognizance.

In the yard, I wanted to do what I had heard others do while incarcerated: burpees. I set a goal of 250, which I could normally complete at home in about twenty-seven to twenty-eight minutes. Unfortunately, it was the earliest yard time I had experienced—around 3:00 or 4:00 p.m.—and the heat and humidity made it difficult. I avoided heatstroke and managed 150 burpees, completely drenched by the end.

By then I had grown used to shouts of "Rusia! Rusia!" whenever someone wanted my attention. A Russian man on the other side of the fence was trying to speak to me—that is how I met Abel. He had been detained for months and knew the system well. He offered to share food or a mug/bowl, which I politely declined, not wanting to be an inconvenience. He also warned me to be careful: one block reportedly had 100 cases of tuberculosis.

A Medical Scare in the Yard

As I walked back to my training spot, I saw Festus from Venezuela—transferred from the same ICE room as I was—leaning on the fence. Suddenly he bent at a ninety-degree angle and dove headfirst into the ground. His forehead left a divot in the clay. He remained like that for what felt like ten to twenty seconds while another man and I shouted, "Help! Help!"

Most staff at Stewart were heavy-set and slow. It took at least thirty seconds to get anyone's attention and another thirty to sixty seconds for them to reach Festus. He regained consciousness, though his face had a strange green-gray color—as if he had been dead. The guards seemed unsure what to do, so I made three trips to the water coolers and brought him three small paper cones of water. It took twenty minutes to get him inside. Although he refused medical attention within a few days he recovered, and soon he was running—and even sprinting—during yard time.

A Cold, a System, and No Response

On Thursday, my cold turned worse—either reaching full strength or newly acquired from someone in the room. I wanted to see a doctor or nurse, but it was nearly impossible. The procedure required submitting a written request on a medical form—one of several supposedly stored in pockets near the pod entrance—but the forms were always missing. Alternatively, I could submit a request via tablet, which I was told usually elicited a quicker response.

I submitted a request, explaining I had a cold with slight fever, headaches, mucus, and that I was essentially blind without contacts or glasses. I also reported intense pain in my left shoulder, with numbness and tingling down my left arm throughout the day and night. The request was ignored.

Frustrated but determined, I tried to sweat it out in the yard. Perhaps exertion and fresh air would help, though I knew it was not ideal.

PART I

Legal Steps, Freezing Intake

Friday morning, I finally spoke with my lawyer. While waiting, I passed one of the detainees in red uniforms—a reminder of the higher-custody population housed elsewhere. Later, I was called with eight other men back to intake to sign for our possessions.

Despite having been issued a jacket on Wednesday or Thursday, we were not allowed to wear or carry it. Intake was freezing, as usual. We spent three hours there; dips on the benches, pacing, and jumping did little to keep the cold at bay. I stared at the clock, read the detainee intake board, and waited my turn. The cold only aggravated my worsening illness.

That afternoon, I made one last attempt to sweat out the sickness—fifty Navy-SEAL-style burpees. It likely had no effect. After midnight, I submitted my commissary order. I prioritized essentials: deodorant, cotton swabs, a mug for liquids, and a bowl for food, plus a few small convenience items—tokens of comfort in an otherwise uncomfortable place.

Commissary and Artificial Scarcity

Saturday passed quietly, though my cold worsened, and sleep was still difficult—headaches, congestion, and relentless mucus. Many detainees had stayed up late Friday night to submit commissary orders, leaving the pod restless and noisy. Commissary orders were accepted only on weekends, and items often sold out quickly. Most products looked like near-expired leftovers from elsewhere, yet they were sold at full price without discount. Friends and family had to keep sending money just to cover these purchases. The entire setup seemed designed less to meet basic needs and more to profit from detainees, creating financial dependence and added stress. The limited stock, inconsistent availability, and inflated prices made one question whether the commissary truly existed for the detainees' benefit—or simply as another revenue stream for the facility.

A Testament in the Yard

During yard time, I walked laps along the fence rather than exercise. I saw Levi again; he said he had obtained a Bible—a Gideons New Testament with Psalms and Proverbs—and promised to bring it to me the next day.

Hoping to "starve" the cold and any infection, I decided to fast from Saturday until Sunday. My eating habits likely seemed strange: I focused only on meat or meat-like items, avoiding beans, rice, and bread. The fasts probably made me seem odd. The only food I looked forward to at Stewart was a dry, slightly chewy cookie—what I thought of as a trailer-park version of a single macaron—served once every three or four days.

Into the Shadows

On Sunday, I skipped and gave away breakfast and lunch. When yard time came, I went out looking for Levi. Thankfully, he spotted me and called my name. Without glasses or contacts, I could not distinguish faces at a distance. We were separated by yard sections, and I did not want him to try to throw the New Testament over the fence.

I asked a guard if a friend (pointing to Levi) could pass me a Bible. He replied that he could not unlock gates or transfer anything himself, but when it came time to leave, I could step into the adjoining section, where it would be allowed to pass the small book through the fence.

That is what we did. Just like that, I finally had something to read—a Gideons New Testament with Psalms and Proverbs. Even though it was the King James Version, it felt like a priceless gift.

Visitors, Not Chaplains

On Monday, a group of visitors came to the pod who looked like chaplains. I had still not seen the actual chaplain associated with Stewart, nor had I received the full Bible I had requested a day or two after arriving. These visitors handed out brochures about hopelessness and suffering, which did not interest me, so I returned to my bunk.

By then, the top bunk next to my boat had been vacated; its occupant had moved to a bottom bunk elsewhere. In that environment, bottom bunks were prime real estate. They made it easier to sit with friends, share a meal, or play games. A man from Eritrea suggested I ask the visitors for a Bible—Russian if possible, or English. I did so. They took down my information and promised to bring one. Later I learned they were not chaplains at all but Jehovah's Witnesses.

I also learned that the Eritrean man had already been held at Stewart for more than a year, with no realistic hope of deportation or release. That same day, another man from a neighboring bottom bunk was wheeled to Medical. His coughing fits had sounded like he was at death's door. Later, word came back that he had been diagnosed with COVID-19.

Tuesday: Voluntary Departure and a Gift

On Tuesday, after breakfast at 6:45 a.m., several of us were called to a meeting with ICE. We waited in a room with twenty or thirty others. After a long stretch, some men asked to use the restroom. The staff pointed them to the staff bathroom, explaining that the detainee restroom was out of order.

It quickly became clear that basic maintenance at Stewart was virtually nonexistent. Much of the facility was in disrepair—sinks, water fountains, several restrooms, and the notorious HVAC system. On our block, one detainee was unofficially tasked with fixing problems, but he had no training and no tools. His efforts usually ended in failure. Our water fountain, for example, stayed wrapped in a paper bag with a bucket underneath to catch the steady leak.

When ICE finally arrived, about an hour into our wait, they presented the option of voluntary departure. Roughly half of the Spanish-speakers signed up on the spot. They had been bounced from one detention center to another for far too long, and many were simply exhausted. Signing meant their case would go before a judge within three or four days, and they would be deported within three to four weeks—with a thousand dollars available to them upon returning to their home country.

I had no interest in this option, but still had to wait for the process to finish before being escorted back to my block.

When I returned, I found a bottle of Sprite and a sleeve of Marías cookies on my bed—a gift from José. The best part was not the soda or cookies but the empty bottle itself. With it, I could finally draw water from the potable tap in the common area instead of relying on the sink taps in the bathroom. That small gift excited me far more than the Sprite.

That day, lunch was served absurdly early—at 10:00 a.m. Afterward, I offered most of the Sprite to Reuben, since I rarely drink soda. What mattered most was keeping the bottle. I set a goal of filling it five or six times a day to stay hydrated, fighting the cold and constant headaches.

Later that morning, my name was called, and I was sent to the Office with one other man. There, the woman overseeing our block handed us Bibles—his in Spanish, mine in English. Mine was the Good News Translation with the Apocrypha. I immediately began reading, finishing Matthew quickly before moving on to Psalms and Proverbs, the books I love most.

A Tragedy in Pod B

That same Tuesday, I learned something terrible. The night before, there had been a commotion outside the pods—shouting, banging, noise that went on for a long while. I had been too tired and sick to pay attention, but now others told me what had happened.

In Pod B, a man had collapsed. He was small and timid, a Spanish-speaker with little English and even fewer resources. His family had no money. During his arrest, ICE officers had beaten him severely. The intake exam—little more than a cursory check—failed to reveal the extent of his injuries, and he was placed in the pod.

But his body could not hold out. He collapsed once, then again, then a third time. Finally, he collapsed a fourth time, in front of everyone. Only then did anyone intervene. Medical staff were called and wheeled him away.

The right side of his body, I was told, was black and blue. His ribs were likely broken, and his liver may have been damaged. The fact that it took four collapses before he was taken seriously was horrifying.

Wednesday: Preparing for Court

On Wednesday, we were given the opportunity to shave. The system was simple: one disposable single-blade razor was exchanged for one ID, and when finished, the razor was returned and the ID was retrieved.

I had not shaved in years, usually trimming with an electric trimmer. But with my bond hearing scheduled for Friday, I wanted to look presentable.

It was slow, painful work. I had three to four weeks of growth, and the cheap razor could barely manage. Every few strokes it clogged, and I had to knock it against the sink to clear it. After twenty minutes of scraping, my towel was speckled with blood. My face burned and stung—I had forgotten how brutal shaving could be with such poor tools.

What struck me most was the kindness of the men around me. There were no real mirrors in the pod—only dull pieces of polished steel bolted to the walls—so others stepped in to help. Some pointed out spots I had missed; others noted where I was bleeding. José offered me his personal mirror. An older man gave me a small bottle of alcohol-based liquid to stop the bleeding. It burned sharply, reminding me of the old days of splashing on Old Spice aftershave. Later, another man came with soothing coconut lotion from the commissary, which eased the burning.

In those small acts of kindness, I felt reassured. Surrounded by strangers, I saw God's care made visible through their concern and generosity.

Thursday: Commissary Day

Thursday is like Christmas in detention—it is commissary day. Orders are placed over the weekend, and on Thursday the delivery finally arrives. For many, it is the one bright spot of the week. And the best part? People share generously, especially with new arrivals.

That morning, however, I was called to Medical—not for the request I had submitted but for the second part of my intake physical. Once again, it was little more than a surface-level check. My blood pressure ("perfect," the nurse said), heart rate, oxygen, and temperature were taken. I weighed in at 177 pounds with clothes on—down another three pounds—and was oddly listed at 5'6½." The nurse even commented that I had good teeth.

When I mentioned that I had been sick with all the typical cold symptoms, the nurse—kind and attentive—took a little more care. She listened to my lungs and heart, then added me to the medicine line, explaining that I would be given liquid medicine now and possibly a combination of liquid medicine and pills later.

Medicine is usually distributed twice a day—morning and evening—but in detention there is no true schedule. Nothing is consistent, and nobody seems to know when the next call will come. It is easy to miss. In fact, I missed the next two nighttime "pill-line/medicina" calls entirely; they took place after midnight, one at 3:00 a.m.

Friday: The Bond Hearing

Friday morning I rose early, skipping breakfast and focusing entirely on the hearing ahead. No one at Stewart had told me what time my hearing would be—not the staff, not the ever-elusive detention officer—but my family said the paperwork listed 8:00 a.m. I showered, brushed my hair, and waited anxiously for my name to be called. At Stewart, nothing was certain.

Abel had warned me the day before: he had been scheduled to meet with his lawyer, but no one came to get him. He spent hours trying to get the staff's attention, and by the time they finally escorted him, his attorney had already tried to call thirteen times—thirteen missed calls. That story stayed with me as I waited.

Thankfully, my name was called with time to spare.

Inside the Courtroom

In the small courtroom, there were three other detainees. One wore a red uniform, and two others sat on the front bench next to me.

The judge began with the two Spanish-speaking men, both requiring an interpreter. Their situations were strikingly similar. Each had entered the country illegally. Each had an American wife and at least one child. Both men were employed and had no criminal history, apart from one who had received a ticket for driving without a license. The judge even paused to deliver a lengthy explanation of why driving without a license was considered a serious offense.

Their attorneys pressed for bond, while the government argued that the court lacked jurisdiction since the men had entered illegally. The judge issued two rulings in each case.

First, she declared that she did not believe she had jurisdiction to grant bond because they had entered illegally. The reaction was heartbreaking: half the courtroom was filled with the first man's family, and they broke down in tears.

Then she issued a second ruling: if a higher court later found that jurisdiction did exist, bond would be set—at roughly $4,500 for each man.

My Turn

I was called next. After confirming that my preferred language was English and that I did not require an interpreter, the record was updated.

The ICE trial attorney (or DHS attorney) began with general questions about my presence in the United States, then shifted to a rapid-fire series of questions I was instructed to answer only with "yes" or "no." To the best of my recollection, these were among them:

- "Have you ever advised or consulted the Russian government?"
- "Have you ever advised or consulted the Russian military?"
- "Have you ever advised or consulted the Wagner Group?"
- "Have you ever advised or consulted the Africa Corps?"
- "Do you have foreign residences?"
- "Do you have foreign bank accounts?"

There may have been more in the same line, but the intent was unmistakable. It was clear to me that DHS—and likely the FBI—believed I was somehow "invisibly" tied to Russia. On the surface, the idea was absurd. Yet it was a dangerous assumption. It had already led to my unlawful detention—effectively a kidnapping and a violation of my rights.

This was not ordinary questioning for a removal proceeding. It felt like something orchestrated from higher levels—a lingering shadow of Russiagate and the obsession with rooting out imagined interference.

The Judge's Ruling

The judge asked the ICE attorney whether she objected to my release on bond. The attorney hesitated, as if trying to conjure a reason, then stated that the burden of proof rested on me to demonstrate why I should be released.

My case was strong: I had entered legally, so jurisdiction was not in question. I had continuous presence, good moral character, and community ties. My attorney argued that the minimum bond of $1,500 was appropriate.

When the judge prepared to rule, she paused. For what felt like an eternity—though it was likely only fifteen seconds—there was silence. In that pause, I prayed.

Finally, she spoke. She granted bond but declared me a high flight risk, setting it at $20,000.

I felt both relief and shock. The amount was far higher than I expected, yet I was grateful. At last, there was a way out.

The Business of Detention

Later, I learned from the men in my pod that very few bonds had been granted in recent months—perhaps one out of a hundred. They had kept this from me so as not to crush my hope.

I also learned that the judge who granted mine had once been known for her fairness in bond hearings but had recently stopped granting them, perhaps under political or administrative pressure from DOJ, DHS, ICE, or other authorities. It became clear that the true goal of these proceedings was not removal or resolution but prolonged detention.

Detention is a business. ICE officers, I was told, had financial incentives to detain. Some said it was $200 per person processed; others speculated it could be as high as $1,500 per head. The exact figure was uncertain, but the point was clear: detention was not about justice, not about immigration, not about the lofty claims made by government agencies. It was about money.

It reminded me of the financial incentives during COVID, when hospitals were paid to admit patients with the virus—and more still for placing them on ventilators.

The Waiting

When I returned to my pod, I felt a strange weight. I wanted to celebrate, but I could not. I had spent only two weeks at Stewart before receiving bond, while many around me had been there for months or even years with no way out and no hope. Many had wives, children, and American families waiting on the outside. I felt guilty that I would soon leave while they remained. I kept the result to myself as long as I could.

The process of leaving on bond is never simple. Someone must physically go to the ICE facility in Atlanta with the money and paperwork. Thankfully, someone was available to help. When I called my family, they told me they already knew and that someone was on the way with the payment.

Then came the next hurdle: ICE bureaucracy. The bond money could not be posted right away because ICE refused to accept it, insisting they first needed a written order from the judge. Hours later, even after the order had been signed, they still refused—this time saying they needed "confirmation from Stewart." No one would give a straight answer about how long the process might take.

This delay was not mere inefficiency—it was built into the system. When a judge orders a detainee's release on bond, ICE has the right to appeal the decision to the Board of Immigration Appeals (BIA). In fact, the appeal process is automatically opened within twenty-four hours of the ruling, giving ICE time to decide whether to challenge the release. They generally have thirty days to file the formal appeal.

What most people do not realize is that ICE can also request an automatic stay of release while their appeal is pending. This means that, even though a judge has already granted bond, ICE can keep a detainee locked up until the BIA rules—essentially turning a bond order into a temporary victory that might never materialize.

As I waited, the silence and vague responses from staff felt deliberate, as though someone was reviewing my case in real time to decide whether my freedom should be challenged. The whole process seemed designed to keep me in limbo just long enough to give ICE the chance to undo the judge's decision.

I had been hopeful—perhaps naïve—thinking I might leave that Friday. In my excitement, I even gave away most of my commissary items. By 5:00 p.m., I knew I would be spending more time in detention. I called my family every hour for updates, but they had nothing encouraging to share. They were just as frustrated as I was.

Saturday: Pain and Prayer

By Saturday, I was counting down the days until Monday—hoping that by then I might finally be released, and that the delay was simply the byproduct of ICE and Stewart's inefficiency. But my sickness took a turn for the worse. The headaches became so persistent that I could barely read my new Bible, though I managed to skim parts of the Apocrypha, which struck me as fun read—similar to fairy tales. I wanted to work out in the yard, but the combination of fever, coughing, and discomfort reduced me to walking slow laps.

That evening, the "pill line" call came at a reasonable hour—between 11:00 p.m. and midnight. We lined up at a barred window, sliding our IDs through and receiving medicine in exchange. I was not sure what the liquid was, but it dried out my sinuses and eased the cough.

Still, sleep was elusive. The lights never turned off, the noise never ceased, and the random singing from showers or the common area carried well into the night. That Saturday it was not the noise but the pain that kept me awake. My head throbbed so badly I could not lie down. I propped myself up on the mattress, but sleep would not come. Around three in the morning, sitting upright with my skull pounding, I prayed—not for anything specific, only for relief.

One of the men—who went by "Shakira," though his real name was Joel —noticed me. He stopped at my bunk and asked, "You can't sleep? Is your head hurting?" I nodded. Without another word, he disappeared and returned with two packets of ibuprofen. I thanked him, swallowed two pills, and waited. The relief came sooner than expected. The headache lifted, and for the first time in days I fell into a deep sleep—so deep I did not stir until the lights brightened for breakfast.

PART I

Sunday: Waiting with Hope

Sunday passed uneventfully, marked mostly by bad food—undercooked diced potatoes seemed to appear at every meal. I ignored the inconveniences and focused on Monday, praying that my bond would finally be accepted and I could leave.

I had also learned that for many detainees, even after bond is granted, payment is sometimes not accepted for days or weeks. And even once accepted, release can be delayed—because of ICE and Stewart's mistakes or because the bond is automatically appealed. It was yet another example of the administrative abuse that had become so normal within ICE and DHS.

Monday: The Day of Release

On Monday morning, I allowed myself a measure of hope. Someone was planning to pay the bond early, and when I called my family after breakfast, I received the good news: the bond had been paid and accepted. Someone was already on the way to Stewart to pick me up.

Stewart only releases detainees between 2:00 and 5:00 p.m., and, like everything else there, the process was slow and riddled with incompetence. The person who came for me arrived promptly at 2:00, only to be told to return at 4:45.

In the meantime, I began giving away what little remained from my commissary order—Q-tips, coffee, headphones, deodorant, and other small items. I gave them to an older Indian man, likely in his late forties or early fifties, who had already spent a month and a half in jail and three months at Stewart. With no family or friends, he was left simply waiting to be deported back to India—a process that often takes six months or more. I admired his positive outlook on life, despite all he had endured.

In detention, he worked sweeping and mopping the pod floors, earning $2 per day. Other jobs paid slightly more—$3 for trash or laundry duty, $4 for work in the cafeteria. The money went into commissary accounts and was returned in cash upon release. When we last spoke, he had $160 saved, which he planned to use for travel from New Delhi to his village once deported.

The entire detention facility depended on men like him to stay operational. Nearly all manual labor was carried out by detainees, paid only a few dollars a day—almost certainly a key factor in keeping the facility profitable for its investors.

I also met a younger Indian man—there were not many from India at Stewart. Desperate for something to read before I had obtained a Bible, he gave me *Cutting for Stone* by Abraham Verghese. We spoke often, and his story was heartbreaking. He had come to the United States legally on a visa, married an American citizen, and together they had a child. He was only a month away from his green card interview when a neighbor called the police.

Through a misunderstanding, he was taken into custody and ended up at Stewart, where he had already spent forty-five days waiting to be reunited with his family.

There was one incident with him that I will never forget. He had been using one of the communal tablets with headphones. When the tablet was misplaced, he became visibly upset and spoke a few frustrated words. Less than two minutes later, the tablet was found. Instead of shrugging it off, he stood before the room, apologized publicly, and then went around to thirty or forty people, shaking hands, looking them in the eye, and expressing regret for his outburst.

This was not the behavior of a "criminal" or "illegal immigrant," as the system claimed to be targeting. It was a picture of humility and decency—a reminder of the humanity so many carried with them, even while being treated as if they had none.

Walking Out

Around 3:00 p.m., a staff member called my name. I was told to pack. As I shoved the bedding, uniform, and issued items into my locker—the blue vinyl bag—I felt a pang of guilt. The men around me began to cheer and clap. There were hugs, fist bumps, and handshakes. As I stepped out, the pod erupted, pounding on the windows in farewell. What made it bittersweet was knowing I was the only one from our block leaving that day.

To my surprise and relief, I encountered Rufus at intake—the man who had helped me settle in when I first arrived. He, too, was leaving, though he had been waiting nearly a week since being granted parole for a year. We sat together in the freezing intake area.

The process was delayed because a woman was being processed nearby. Stewart did not permit men and women to mix, and this was the first time I had seen a woman there, even from a distance. Only after she was finished were we called to sign paperwork, collect commissary balances, and retrieve our phones

My friend, who had arrived hours earlier, was told to return at 4:45 p.m. But in typical Stewart fashion, the staff changed the time again—this time to 7:00. When I finally stepped outside the gates just after 5:00, my friend had already left. I called him, and he promised to return in five minutes.

Standing at the gate with a guard beside me, phone in hand, I felt a strange stillness settle over me. A quiet realization came: this part of my journey was over.

PART I

God's Faithfulness

Through it all, God had been with me. Despite the hardships, waiting, and uncertainty, He kept me safe—and even in weakness, mostly healthy.

"And we know that for those who love God all things work together for good, for those who are called according to His purpose" (Romans 8:28).

This is not a trite slogan but a profound declaration of God's providence. It assures believers that no event—however bitter—is wasted in His economy. For those who love Him and are called by Him, everything—whether seen as blessing or trial—is being woven into a tapestry of eternal good, with Christ at the center.

Epilogue: Strength in Weakness

Walking out of Stewart was not simply the end of my detention; it was the beginning of a deeper awareness of God's providence. I had prayed countless times for release, and when the door finally opened, I understood more fully that His timing is never late, though it often feels slow to us.

At Stewart, even the nights had been made uncomfortable. On at least two occasions, the temperature inside our pod was turned up to what felt like the high seventies, possibly the low eighties. It was done while people were trying to sleep, and in that kind of heat rest was almost impossible. Those who managed to doze off often woke up again, their uniforms, sheets, and thin blankets sticking to their bodies. Each time the door opened, the rush of air from the hallway felt freezing by comparison, a reminder that even the thermostat could be used to control us.

Stepping outside after release, the contrast struck me in a different way. It was mid-August, warm and humid, yet as I stood with the gate guard waiting for the outer gate to open and for my friend to arrive, I felt goosebumps rise on my arms. The moment was so surreal that it felt almost otherworldly. After weeks of confinement, I was finally outside, and the weight of control had been lifted. In that instant, I sensed more clearly than ever that freedom is not granted by men but by God alone. The goosebumps were not from the air but from the realization that His hand had carried me through, and that He had answered prayers in His perfect time.

Yet even in freedom, I carried with me the faces and names of men who remained behind—fathers, husbands, sons—still waiting without hope, caught in a system designed to grind them down. Their kindness and generosity, even in suffering, deepened my compassion and gave me a clearer picture of Christ's words: *"I was in prison and you came to me"* (Matthew 25:36).

If there is one lesson detention etched into my heart, it is that weakness is not failure. Weakness is the very place where God's strength becomes visible. What I endured was not wasted—it became a testimony of His faithfulness.

And as Paul wrote, "When I am weak, then I am strong" (2 Corinthians 12:10).

In truth, there was absolutely nothing I could do to help myself in that situation. My fate was in the hands of God, who in His providence chose even flawed human instruments to carry out His purposes. Stripped of every illusion of control, I learned that my deliverance would come only from Him. So too the psalmist declares:

> "Blessed are those whose strength is in You,
>   in whose heart are the highways to Zion.
> As they go through the Valley of Baca
>   they make it a place of springs;
> the early rain also covers it with pools.
> They go from strength to strength;
>   each one appears before God in Zion."
> (Psalm 84:5–7)

What the world calls weakness, God turns into strength. What feels like a barren valley becomes, by His grace, a place of springs. And every trial and every moment of waiting leads His children from strength to strength—until at last they stand before Him in Zion.

Wednesday - Part 2 - The Home Visit

When I returned home, I learned two unsettling details about the Wednesday of my arrest. That morning, my father had driven to a prayer meeting in the Lexus I usually used. On the way to Perimeter Church, he noticed a car trailing him. When he parked, the vehicle stopped at a distance, clearly observing who would step out of the Lexus. Sensing the unusual attention, my father lingered outside the church, hoping to see who was following him —but no one ever emerged.

Later that day, Cwieka appeared at the house with the white female FBI agent—the same one who had been in the room with me earlier. He pounded on the door, rang the bell repeatedly, and when he spotted my brother through the small front window, sneered, "I'm gonna take him."

Cwieka: "Don't answer the f***ing door."
Female agent: "What's he doing?"
Cwieka: "He is coming down."
Female agent: "Oh s***."
Cwieka: "I'm gonna take him."
Female agent: "Oh s***, a brother?"

PART I

Cwieka: "Yeah."
Female agent: "F***."
Cwieka: "It's all right."

The female agent laughed. When no one answered, they waited.

Not long after, when my father returned home, Cwieka confronted him directly. The agents, in plain clothes, never introduced themselves. Instead, Cwieka declared that my father should be grateful he was doing him a "huge favor" by delivering the Notices to Appear in person—reminding him that he and my mother were not in a cell like their son. Then, with mocking cruelty, he added: "…put you in a cell next to Kirill… If you want, I can take you downtown, you can sit in a cell next to him if you want?"

The documents he handed over were another fiasco: both were duplicates of my mother's Notice to Appear. Whether through incompetence or a deliberate attempt to make my father miss his hearing, it was yet another example of DHS and ICE bungling—or manipulating—the process. Later, when names were checked against the court docket, my father discovered that he also had a scheduled hearing.

Cwieka then produced an iPhone confiscated over a year earlier. But it was not to return it. Instead, he claimed my father's lawyer had asked to retrieve some phone numbers from it. When my father requested the phone, Cwieka deflected, insisting there was a procedure, and ominously adding: "But there is still that one image on there. I don't know, it's in…" His vague, unfinished remark cast suspicion without clarity—a tactic of intimidation and manipulation.

Cwieka: "Okay, so, I have your phone so that you can get phone numbers, your lawyer said you wanted to get some phone numbers off of it. Is that true or no?"
Father: "What lawyer said?"
Cwieka: "Your lawyer. Umm…"
Father: "Lawyer said what?"
Cwieka: "Jay… that you wanted to get some phone numbers off of it."
Father: "I want my phone."
Cwieka: "Oh! No. He said, well he said you wanted phone numbers off of it."
Father: "No, I want my phone."
Cwieka: "Okay. So, what we're gonna do is send notice then that you can come and get it. Probably. But there is still that one image on there, I don't know, it's in…"
Father: "No, no. No. I told you I want my phone back."
Cwieka: "I am just telling you what he told me. All right, I am not trying to be confrontational with you. If you wanna be confrontational, I'll be confrontational also. Okay, I am trying to be fair with you. Regardless. This

is the paperwork I was told to give for your phone. iPhone 7 with your serial number, here's instructions on what you need to do if you wanna get it back."
Father: "No."
Cwieka: "No what?"
Father: "If I can't get my phone back, you can keep it."
Cwieka: "These are instructions on what you need to do to get it back. If you wanna get it back. If you don't…"
Father: "I don't need it."
Cwieka: "Okay, um, well I'm, I'm gonna leave this with you."

Adding to the web of lies, Cwieka claimed he had seen me but "hadn't gotten the chance" to speak with me. That, too, was false. Before leaving, he once again pressed my father for information that did not exist, chasing shadows of his own imagination:

Cwieka: "I… I want you to know though, in case you find yourself in a bad spot, there are people you could talk to if you wanted to. To help your situation out. No? No?"
Father: "No."
Cwieka: "Okay."
Female agent: "All right."
Cwieka: "Thank you."

A Calculated Assault on Family

There is perhaps no greater way to inflict emotional devastation on a family than to kidnap or unlawfully arrest their eldest son and then attempt to do the same to the youngest—especially in the presence of aging parents. This is not merely bureaucratic overreach; it is cruelty calculated to maximize fear, anxiety, and helplessness. It recalls some of history's darkest moments—the rounding up of people based solely on their identity, race, or origin—acts that civilized nations have since condemned as unjust and inhumane.

After that Wednesday, my family lived in constant dread. They were afraid to leave the house, scanning the street for unmarked cars, bracing for more pounding on the door, more threats, and the possibility of yet another disappearance. What happened to us was not just a procedural failure; it was an assault on human dignity that weaponized fear as a tool of control.

When I was arrested, I was not asked for my name or identification, and there was no questioning. These men knew who I was because they had been tracking me, stalking me, and my family—not because any of us were criminals, but because of our nationality and origin. In that moment, it became clear that this was not law enforcement acting on a tip or a random encounter; this was a planned operation designed for maximum control and shock value.

PART I

    This behavior is not merely bureaucratic clumsiness; it is targeted harassment. My father—a sixty-nine-year-old ordained minister with a history of multiple heart attacks, open-heart surgery, and multiple stent procedures—was subjected to physical and emotional abuse in his own home. The pounding on the door, the shouted threats, the taunting offer to "put you in a cell next to Kirill," the manipulation of paperwork and electronic devices, and the blatant disregard for his medical condition meet every element of elder abuse under O.C.G.A. § 30-5-4(a). They also satisfy the legal criteria for intentional infliction of emotional distress: deliberate conduct, outrageous behavior, causation, and severe emotional harm—including chest pains later confirmed by his physician to be an anterior infarct. Cwieka's actions were not an accident or a misunderstanding—they were part of a sustained pattern of harassment designed to break a family's will.

    "Woe to those who devise wickedness and work evil on their beds! When the morning dawns, they perform it, because it is in the power of their hand."
—Micah 2:1

    This is the spirit in which too many in positions of authority operate. They act not according to what is just or lawful, but according to what they can get away with, unafraid of accountability. They remain in power despite a well-documented record of incompetence and abuse. They fabricate villains, construct conspiracies, and twist narratives—not to protect America, but to justify their budgets, their jobs, and their relevance.

From the Soviet Union to Russiagate

This is not a new tactic. Under the Soviet regime, Evangelicals were branded as American spies; today, in the United States, they are smeared as Russian agents. The irony could not be more bitter. And yet the same machinery continues to churn—still clinging to the ghost of Russiagate. That entire affair was a hoax, a colossal waste of time and resources, but rather than admit failure, federal agencies search for new names to attach to the same debunked narrative. Russophobia stalks the halls of government, not as a matter of national security but as a partisan weapon, a convenient way to revive old crusades rather than do real law enforcement.

    The questioning I faced at ICE was narrowly focused on Russian "operations." Later, at my bond hearing, the questions again centered on Russia—its military, its security services, its supposed networks of influence. Combined with the relentless interrogations of my father, it is obvious that this was never about administrative process. It was an attempt to redeem a failed political narrative, to justify years of wasted manpower and expense by manufacturing another target.

Instead of a routine adjustment of status—ordinarily resolved in three to six months—this process was stretched into more than six years, stealing time, draining finances, hindering ministry, and coercing my parents into medical decisions they would not otherwise have made. This is not merely delay; it is abuse. USCIS must now adjudicate the pending I-485 based on the facts as they existed in 2020—before this malicious delay turned into a vehicle for intelligence-gathering and narrative-building.

Meanwhile, the FBI has dragged this case through at least three abeyances, producing nothing of substance. It has been more than four years since my parents' interview and over five years since the application was filed. The fishing expedition must end. The proper response from DHS, USCIS, and the FBI would be simple: acknowledge the abuse, apologize, and ask, *"What can we do to make this right?"*

Officials who perpetuate this abuse are not neutral actors. They are relics of failed political crusades—partisan weapons masquerading as guardians of justice. Their worldview is twisted and misaligned, shaped by bias and self-preservation rather than truth. Many are holdovers from prior administrations, still operating on outdated intelligence, still pursuing expired agendas, and in some cases actively undermining the current administration because their own promotions were tied to its predecessor. Such people should no longer hold positions of power—not as an act of retribution, but as a matter of responsible governance. America deserves better than an FBI or DHS led by Russophobic officials and operatives who exploit the mantle of law enforcement to settle old political scores.

Yet even here, amid injustice, Romans 8:28 reminds us of God's unshakable sovereignty:

"And we know that for those who love God all things work together for good,
for those who are called according to his purpose."

This is not a hollow promise that every hardship will feel good or be quickly reversed. It is the assurance that nothing—not persecution, not injustice, not state power—can derail God's plan. My prayer is that America learns from this moment: that justice delayed is not justice at all, and that its power must never be used to punish those who have already suffered for the sake of their faith.

In the weeks that followed, as the fragments came together, I saw what truly stood behind my arrest. It had begun years earlier, when my father's ministry drew the wrong kind of attention—when faith itself became the evidence and devotion to God was treated as subversion of the state, first under the Soviets and now under their ideological heirs. My arrest was not an isolated event but the continuation of that same pattern—an inheritance of suspicion, the next movement in a long and uneasy composition.

PART II
Faith at a Price

PART II

In the gray years of the Soviet Union—when truth was rationed and fear mistaken for loyalty—rebellion did not always come with banners or speeches. Sometimes it began quietly: a refusal to bow, to sign, or to conform.

Two brothers, Alexander and Kirill Podrabinek, were raised by their widowed father, Pinkhos, a Jewish man who taught them to think freely and bow only before God. Like their classmates, they joined the Young Pioneers, for in those years such conformity was expected. But when the time came to enter the Komsomol—the youth arm of the Communist Party—they refused.

It was a small act, almost invisible amid the machinery of obedience. Yet in a nation where conformity was counted as virtue, omission became rebellion. They were the only two in their school who would not enlist. Confused administrators could only conclude one of two things: either they were Baptists, or they were enemies of the state. According to Soviet logic, they were both.

That quiet defiance became the first note in a larger symphony of conscience—a faint but growing sound against the static of propaganda. It was not yet a movement, only a murmur, but it reminded a silenced nation that freedom still had a voice.

As he grew older, Alexander longed to heal. Barred from medical school because of his "unreliable" background, he trained instead as a paramedic—a profession the regime considered harmless enough for a mind it mistrusted. Yet the door the state had closed became the one through which his conscience would walk into history.

Inside Soviet medicine, Alexander discovered a deeper sickness. Psychiatry had been weaponized; dissent itself had been reclassified as mental illness. Believers, thinkers, and critics were diagnosed as delusional and confined as patients. Truth had become a symptom of disease.

He began to document what he saw—names, dates, methods, medications—and smuggled his reports to the West. His evidence exposed a cruelty cloaked in compassion, revealing how medicine, meant to heal, had been made to serve ideology. For this, the state branded him an enemy of the people. He was arrested, interrogated, and exiled. But his words outlived his imprisonment, crossing borders to expose what the Soviet Union feared most: that tyranny often wears a humanitarian face.

In time, Alexander Podrabinek stood among others whose courage made truth visible again—men like Andrei Sakharov and Natan Sharansky, who in different ways resisted the same machine of deception and control.

Sakharov, the father of the Soviet hydrogen bomb, once wielded the power to destroy the world. In that power, he glimpsed the moral ruin of the nation that had created it. He turned from weapons to words, from scientific mastery to moral clarity. For speaking of human dignity and freedom, he was stripped of honors, exiled, and silenced. His genius had made him indispensable; his conscience made him intolerable.

Sharansky, a mathematician and Jewish activist, sought only the freedom to live honestly—to think, speak, and emigrate as a man should. For that, he became a refusenik, then a prisoner. In 1977, under KGB chief Yuri Andropov, he was accused of treason for allegedly passing names of Jewish believers to the West—a lie punishable by death. He spent thirteen years in the gulag. His crime was to live in truth.

Each of these men faced the same adversary—not merely the Soviet regime, but the moral architecture of deceit that sustained it. They fought on different fronts—Sakharov in science, Sharansky in ideology, Podrabinek in medicine—yet their cause was one: to defend the integrity of the human soul against a system built to erase it.

Their defiance proved that even in an empire founded on lies, conscience cannot be nationalized and truth cannot be made a servant of the state. Yet for every name history remembers, there were thousands more who stood quietly—men and women whose courage was never recorded, whose faith was tested in prisons, factories, and whispered prayers.

These were the people who shaped my parents' world—believers who refused to lie even when silence might have saved them. Their courage revealed what every empire fears most: that truth cannot be legislated, and conscience cannot be chained.

Mother

It was in this same climate of suspicion and quiet resistance that my mother was born—the youngest of four daughters in a Christian family that lived their faith at great risk. She was baptized at eighteen, knowing that even such a simple act could draw the attention of the authorities.

The government's chief concern was not private belief, but the gathering of believers. Agents were posted at bus stops and train stations, ready to intercept those traveling to worship services that often had to be held in remote villages outside Moscow. Even when believers recognized one another along the way, they avoided acknowledgment, fearful of alerting the ever-watchful eyes that followed them.

Approaching a gathering of believers was always an act of courage. The state stationed both uniformed officers and plainclothes agents near every suspected meeting place. Members of the KGB and their informants loitered in unmarked cars, stood in doorways, and watched from the shadows—ready to question, detain, or intimidate anyone who passed by. Believers learned to recognize them: the same faces lingering too long, the same cars idling without purpose. They sang their hymns with one eye on the door.

The streets themselves pulsed with suspicion. In apartment buildings, neighbors listened through thin walls, ready to report an "enemy of the state" for a few rubles or a favor. In such a world, faith could never be casual.

Every hymn, every sermon, every whispered prayer was an act of defiance. To worship was to risk everything—and yet they met, and they worshiped.

During those same years, my mother came of age amid vigilance and quiet courage. Within her Baptist community, she learned early that following Christ meant being watched, recorded, and reported. Police raids were frequent, especially at gatherings of young believers. Students were singled out for punishment; universities were instructed to expel anyone identified as Christian.

Every student carried a student ticket—an identification card required for university entry and discounted travel on Moscow's public transport. It was more than a pass; it was the key to education, mobility, and the future. Losing it meant the end of one's studies, and with it, the end of opportunity. My mother, a diligent student living on a modest forty-ruble stipend, could not afford such a loss. Yet attending worship always put that ticket at risk.

Before each gathering, she would slip it under the insole of her boot—a small act of foresight and faith. Once, when police stormed a youth service and threw her into the back of a patrol car, she had only seconds to hide it beneath her heel. That night, as the car sped through the dark, she pressed her foot down hard, praying they would not search her shoes.

On other occasions, the young believers were rounded up and loaded onto buses, then taken "beyond the 100th kilometer"—sixty miles or more past the road encircling Moscow. They would be unloaded in the middle of the forest, left to find their way home through the snow or mud, hoping to catch the last train back to the city around one in the morning.

In a world where faith itself was a liability, that hidden ticket became a symbol of something larger: the determination to hold on to both truth and hope, to protect what little freedom remained. For believers like her, every gathering was a declaration that the soul could not be confiscated—and that even under tyranny, worship was still worth the risk.

Among those young believers was Alexander Podrabinek, invited to attend one of their meetings to bear witness to the risks Christians faced and to speak on the growing persecution of faith across the Soviet Union. His presence was an act of solidarity—but it also made the gathering a target.

As expected, the *militsiya*, assisted by *druzhinniki*—civilian enforcers who served the regime for small favors—raided the meeting. These men were not trained officers but opportunists, trading conscience for the Party favor. They were the blunt instruments of a fearful state, the human extensions of a bureaucracy without mercy.

That night, several young believers were arrested—among them my mother, her sister, and Alexander. They were interrogated, threatened, and briefly imprisoned. Yet their faith did not break. What the state mistook for weakness—worship, prayer, and fellowship—was, in truth, their strength.

The atheist regime understood that the surest way to destroy faith was to sever its roots in the next generation. It sought to isolate the children and youth from any exposure to religion, calling faith "the opium of the mind." Attendance at church by minors was strictly forbidden. Pastors were ordered not to baptize the young and were pressured to report any students who appeared in services to the authorities. Religion was treated as a contagion to be contained, and the faithful as carriers of infection.

Because of this, correspondence between believers was watched closely. When Alexander was later sentenced to internal exile, my mother began sending him small parcels—food, warm clothing, and simple reminders that the righteous are never forgotten. To protect her from surveillance, my grandmother signed the parcel slips in her own name, and Alexander addressed his letters to her instead. It was an unspoken code—a quiet act of defiance that allowed faith to flow where fear tried to stop it.

My mother still keeps one of those letters. Its paper has yellowed with age, its ink faded, but its spirit unbroken—a quiet testimony from a time when truth was treason and faith a criminal act. It remains a reminder that even under the shadow of empire, conscience still spoke, and hope still found a way to endure.

Father

Out of that crucible of persecution, my father found his calling—to serve, to lead, and to bear witness to a truth no government could suppress. The same spirit that had moved men like Sakharov, Sharansky, and Podrabinek—the spirit that taught my mother to hide her student ticket beneath her boot and sing hymns in defiance of fear—shaped him as well.

He, too, was born into a Christian family in the Soviet Union—a quiet household of faith surrounded by suspicion. Like many of his generation, he grew up knowing that belief in God was not merely unfashionable; it was forbidden. Yet from that forbidden faith would rise the purpose of his life.

After completing his mandatory service in the Soviet Army, he came to personal faith in Jesus Christ in 1978. Just weeks later, his newfound devotion was tested. He was arrested, brutally interrogated, and pressured to renounce his faith—but he refused.

As a brand-new believer, he endured imprisonment, physical torment, and threats from inmates who were encouraged to break him. Yet even there, behind the iron bars of a system built to silence conscience, he prayed, sang hymns (often out of tune), and shared the Gospel with anyone who would listen. His cell became his pulpit; his endurance, a living sermon.

Though eventually released, persecution followed him like a shadow. About a year later, he was arrested again—this time for defending his sister during a church service that had been interrupted by police. That detention would unexpectedly draw international attention. His sister Natalia, along with my mother Luba (then his future wife) and Luba's sister Vera, reached out to Academician Andrei Sakharov, who by then had become the moral conscience of a restless empire.

Sakharov relayed their story to Voice of America and Radio Free Europe, which broadcast the names of every detainee across the airwaves, briefly making them known throughout the West. At trial, the judge accused them of being "American spies"—a familiar Soviet tactic that cast faith as treason and conscience as subversion.

But light exposed what fear sought to hide. Instead of the long sentences they feared, they were released after twenty days—likely because the Brezhnev regime, already faltering under its own contradictions, feared the outcry of the international press.

Upon his release, a church elder gave my father simple but prophetic advice: learn English. He took it to heart, not realizing how deeply that decision would shape his future. In 1982, he met a man serving in the American diplomatic corps in Moscow who also directed Campus Crusade for Christ's ministry in Russia. Because my father was one of the few Russian believers fluent in English, he became a vital partner in the ministry —a bridge between Western missionaries and the persecuted church behind the Iron Curtain.

His life, like those who came before him, was a quiet act of defiance—a living declaration that faith cannot be banned, truth cannot be silenced, and conscience will not bow.

By 1989, my father was leading Campus Crusade's New Life Training Center, a ministry focused on showing the Jesus Film and teaching the Four Spiritual Laws. Under his leadership, one training center became three. Though worn down by state opposition and constant risk, my father, with my mother's support, pressed forward, convinced that the Gospel was worth every cost.

In 1990, the November/December issue of *Worldwide Challenge*— Campus Crusade's magazine—published an article about my father titled *The Reluctant Evangelist*, referring to him as "Petya," a man who often felt like "a squeezed lemon" from the strain of sharing the Gospel. I remember those days well. Though he was a loving and devoted father, he would come home visibly drained. Most of the time we had together was spent at Bible studies or on the streets of Moscow where he evangelized. His Arbat Street evangelism, which began in 1987, took a heavy toll on both him and my mother. By that point he had already been arrested five times, and a sixth arrest would have meant a mandatory prison term. My mother and grandmother pleaded with him to stop—but he would not.

Out of persecution came purpose. The same faith that had sustained my father through prison walls became the foundation for everything that followed. Hardship had refined him, stripping away fear and hesitation until only conviction remained. Each arrest had tested his resolve; each release only deepened his sense of calling. He came to believe that true freedom was

Faith at a Price

not the absence of danger but the presence of the Gospel—and that if God could open hearts behind iron bars, He could also open doors across a nation.

That conviction soon took form in a vision larger than survival: to build, not merely to endure; to plant churches, not just defend them; to train leaders who would carry the Gospel into places he himself might never reach.

Building Churches and Bridges

In the early 1990s, my father set out to formally organize a church that would welcome new believers, naming it Novogireevo after the nearest Metro station. In 1991, he officially registered the Center for Evangelism in Russia later renamed to Russian Association of Independent Evangelical Churches (RAIEC). In 1995 Perimeter Church founded the Russian Center for Church Multiplication (RCCM) in the United States. Perimeter Church played a key role in RCCM's founding, helping to create an independent board of ministry leaders from across the country to oversee the organization. At its first meeting on December 1, 1995, the board resolved to establish RCCM as a nonprofit corporation under section 501(c)(3) of the Internal Revenue Code. RAIEC and RCCM went on to plant forty-six Evangelical churches across Russia.

Recognizing that simply planting churches with nominal converts was not enough, my father pursued formal theological training, entering the master's program at Gordon-Conwell Theological Seminary in July 1997 and earning his Doctor of Ministry in 2004. By August 2000, RCCM's mission had matured into a strategy of evangelism, pastoral training, and church multiplication. As Russian government restrictions tightened — often under the influence of the Russian Orthodox Church, which viewed Evangelicals as foreign intruders — RCCM added a new approach: building relationships with political leaders, sharing the Gospel with them, and demonstrating how Evangelical churches could serve communities and government alike.

The real opposition came from Russian elites, who viewed Evangelicals as agents of American influence. My father suggested that instead of avoiding these power centers, RCCM should engage them directly. He proposed using the Russian National Prayer Breakfast (RNPB) as a bridge to Russia's political and business leaders. The board was initially hesitant and unfamiliar with the RNPB — or even the U.S. National Prayer Breakfast (USNPB) — but through persistence and prayer, doors eventually opened. My father was elected chairman of the RNPB board and later became its president. He reshaped the event to better engage Russia's leaders, mentored new Christian leaders, and built bridges between church figures and government officials. This work gave Evangelicals greater legitimacy and space to operate.

For a time, it seemed as though the long years of suffering had given way to fruit. The work that began in secret apartments under Soviet surveillance now found open doors in government halls, universities, and churches. My father had learned to speak the language of faith to those in power, showing that the Gospel could bridge divides the Cold War had carved deep. His calling, once confined to underground worship, had grown into a mission that touched diplomats and dignitaries alike.

Yet the same ministry that opened hearts in Russia would, years later, draw suspicion in America. The nation that had once prayed for persecuted believers behind the Iron Curtain began to view them through the lens of politics and fear. What God had used to reconcile enemies would soon be recast as evidence of collusion.

History has a way of repeating itself in unexpected places. In the Soviet Union, a regime that declared God dead and religion a poison hunted my parents for their faith. They were watched, questioned, and punished simply because they worshiped Christ. Yet today—on the soil of a nation that proclaims its Christian heritage, cites Scripture in its founding documents, and sends missionaries across the world—my parents once again found themselves surveilled and targeted by another government for practicing the very same faith. The irony is painful: the persecution they survived in an atheistic regime resurfaced in a country that boasts of its religious freedom.

Suspicion in America

What my parents endured under Soviet persecution became their preparation for the trials to come—not in Moscow, but in America. For the shadow of tyranny does not die with an empire; it only learns a new language.

In February 2008, at the USNPB, my father met Alexander Torshin, a prominent Russian politician who became a strong supporter of the RNPB. By March, my father was hosting parliamentary breakfasts and inviting senior officials, using the platform to evangelize, promote moral values, and raise advocates for religious freedom within Russia's government.

During the Russiagate era, U.S. agencies — under immense political pressure — seized on Maria Butina as proof of Russian influence operations. She had attended the RNPB in 2015 as a guest of Torshin — a tenuous connection that nevertheless placed my father in the periphery of the investigation. Between August 16–18, 2015, Torshin visited Atlanta, attended several Evangelical churches, and met with leaders from Perimeter Church, North Point Community Church, and Passion City Church. On April 30, 2017, journalist Tom Hamburger published a *Washington Post* article naming my father — potentially flagging him for federal agencies. From that point forward, the scrutiny intensified.

Butina was arrested on July 15, 2018, and in December of that year, she pled guilty to conspiring to act as an unregistered foreign agent. She was released and deported in October 2019. Just weeks earlier, on August 19, 2019, Netflix released *The Family*, which featured an interview with my father — placing him and his work in the public eye at a time when suspicion toward Russian nationals was at its peak.

In truth, my father's leadership of the RNPB was a biblically mandated ministry endeavor. His goal was to evangelize Russian politicians and elites, fostering a spiritual reformation of Russia's leadership for the sake of the nation's future — and the world's future. But instead of being recognized as a minister pursuing a religious mission, he was cast under suspicion. Federal agencies, misunderstanding both Russian history and my father's personal story, treated his ministry as inherently suspect. This politically motivated scrutiny culminated in a series of FBI-requested abeyances amounting to a five-year suspension — without explanation — of my parents' Green Card applications after the 2021 interviews. This came as a shock to both my parents and their attorney. Since then, my father and those connected to him have been subjected to repeated questioning and intrusive investigations — efforts less concerned with truth than with fishing for political contacts and leveraging a narrative of Russian interference.

What began as misunderstanding soon hardened into something far more deliberate. Bureaucratic caution turned to fixation; administrative inquiry became suspicion. The same government that once welcomed refugees of persecution now mirrored the tactics of the regimes they fled—question first, justify later, and presume guilt where none exists. For my father, the scrutiny that began with whispers and paperwork soon took a physical form. Agents who saw politics in every prayer and conspiracy in every act of faith turned his ministry into a pretext for interrogation. What followed was not oversight —it was harassment dressed in the language of national security.

Shadows of Russiagate

Even though the Trump administration consistently maintained that Russiagate was a politically motivated hoax — exaggerated and manufactured to discredit Donald Trump — the shadow of that narrative has never lifted. DHS, the FBI, and USCIS treated my parents' Green Card applications not as routine adjustments of status but as opportunities for intelligence-gathering, dragging the process out for years. Instead of adjudicating their case on its merits, federal agents subjected them to needless delay, repeated interrogations, and unjust suspicion — keeping the ghost of Russiagate alive at their expense.

This campaign of harassment became personal on November 15, 2022, when my father was stopped for his first airport interrogation. The questioning lasted roughly three hours. John Cwieka, the DHS special agent who led the interrogation, sneered that my father did not "look like a pastor." On the table before them sat what may have been a real — or fabricated — large stack of paperwork, intended to intimidate and create the impression of a case file full of incriminating evidence. Yet despite this display, Cwieka and his associates failed to see what was obvious: my father's decades-long record of ministry and documented persecution in Russia. Every arrest, every court appearance, and every risk he took bore witness to his faith and his calling — not to espionage or political intrigue.

The questioning focused on two primary areas. Roughly an hour was spent probing my father about his contacts in Russian and American politics, followed by another hour of repeated questions specifically about Alexander Torshin and Maria Butina. The remaining time was devoted to scrutinizing the details of how my father financed his international travel.

Weeks later, on January 26, 2023, *The Washington Post* published another article revisiting the Butina case, again linking the National Prayer Breakfast to alleged Russian influence operations. This renewed public attention coincided with escalating federal scrutiny of my father and those associated with him.

On September 12, 2023, this campaign escalated when a senior pastor of a large Slavic evangelical church in Atlanta was ambushed and interrogated by two federal agents—one identified by the pastor as John Cwieka from DHS, and the other from the FBI. Although USCIS has the authority to conduct administrative site visits as part of compliance reviews, such visits are normally brief, conducted by a single USCIS immigration officer, and limited in scope. What occurred here was neither routine nor administrative. It was a prolonged, adversarial interrogation by a DHS special agent and an FBI agent—carried out without notice, without allowing the pastor to bring an interpreter or legal counsel, and without a warrant or subpoena.

This pastor, an American citizen and the founding leader of a church that has consistently championed pro-American values, was subjected to tactics that bypassed the ordinary constitutional safeguards owed to citizens. Under the U.S. Constitution, interrogations by federal law enforcement require judicial process—typically a warrant or subpoena—and must be conducted in a manner that respects civil rights. Instead, under the guise of a compliance review, two agents exploited the pastor's vulnerabilities—his limited English proficiency and his speech impediment—to subject him to a process he was ill-equipped to navigate. This was not a compliance review; it was an intelligence-gathering operation masquerading as an administrative visit.

Because of the pastor's difficulty with English, the agents struggled to understand his responses—yet they nevertheless documented their own interpretation of what was said. Their version of events, later cited in the Notice of Intent to Revoke my father's petition, mischaracterized and distorted much of the conversation. Their conclusions revealed a fundamental ignorance of church operations and nonprofit governance, producing a misleading and damaging record.

Less than two months later, on February 5, 2024, a senior elder at a major church in Atlanta, who also directed RCCM, was questioned by

Cwieka and another agent believed to be with the FBI. During this interrogation, Cwieka was once again explicitly identified by name: "John."

Then, on February 19, 2024, my father endured yet another ordeal. He was returning from Moscow to the United States, a grueling journey that, due to sanctions, required a layover in Istanbul and more than 24 hours of travel time, including 17 hours in the air without meaningful rest. I waited for more than three and a half hours at the airport arrivals area, but my father never came out with the other passengers. No one from the airline, airport, or federal authorities offered any information about his whereabouts.

My father is in his late sixties and has a long, serious medical history: multiple heart attacks, an open-heart surgery (quadruple bypass) — I still vividly recall seeing him unconscious in the recovery room, tubes protruding from his body — and an additional procedure requiring stents. Even after direct flights, he was visibly exhausted and often needed several days to recover. On this occasion, however, there would be no recovery period. Instead of being allowed rest, he was again detained and subjected to a four-hour interrogation by Cwieka and another federal agent, this time late into the night.

The questioning focused almost exclusively on his "political connections": who he met with, when, and why. My father explained that the individuals he met with were attendees of the Russian National Prayer Breakfast — men and women he was ministering to as part of his calling. His electronic devices were seized despite earlier searches revealing nothing. Cwieka even promised to personally return the devices the next day — a promise he never kept. It took months before my father recovered some of them. Before releasing him, Cwieka remarked that they knew where both of his sons were — referring specifically to my brother and me — and that we were being watched and tracked.

This late-night interrogation placed an extraordinary burden on a man who was already physically compromised from prolonged travel and chronic health issues. The timing and method of this encounter were not incidental — they were deliberate and calculated. As with every prior interaction, Cwieka's approach relied on intimidation, threats, and a calculated disregard for due process and basic decency. His goal was unmistakable: to place my father, and by extension my family, at the greatest possible disadvantage, extracting fragments of information that could be twisted to fit a pre-constructed, politically motivated narrative.

The pattern was unmistakable. What began as isolated encounters had become a campaign—calculated, sustained, and increasingly lawless. Each interrogation stripped away another layer of pretense, revealing not an investigation in pursuit of truth but an operation driven by fear and pride. Behind every late-night questioning and every withheld document stood a system willing to break its own laws to defend its errors. What had once been personal injustice now stood as public evidence of something deeper—an institutional betrayal of the very freedoms it claimed to protect.

And yet, through every act of intimidation, one truth endured: no government can silence what God has already vindicated. The same hand that permitted trial also preserved witness, turning each assault on faith into testimony for the truth itself.

Legal and Human Costs

This campaign revealed more than misconduct; it exposed the quiet unraveling of principle. By targeting a minister for engaging with political leaders, federal agents violated the very Constitution they swore to uphold. The First Amendment's guarantees of free exercise and religious independence were set aside, chilling protected ministry and burdening sacred work without cause.

Their repeated, notice-free interrogations—administrative visits turned adversarial inquests—bypassed the Fifth Amendment's due process protections, replacing law with intimidation. Under the Religious Freedom Restoration Act (RFRA), any federal action that burdens religious exercise must be the least restrictive means of pursuing a compelling government interest. No such interest was ever shown. Fear, not necessity, drove their conduct. Delay and harassment became tools of control—not to uncover truth, but to sustain a political illusion.

The five-year "abeyance" of my parents' I-485 applications—paired with interrogations that sought intelligence rather than adjudication—was not administration but manipulation. Immigration law became theater: a stage upon which suspicion was rehearsed, and time itself weaponized to extract what evidence could not supply.

The human cost was severe. Subjecting a sixty-nine-year-old man with a fragile heart to this pattern of harassment inflicted real physical and emotional harm—pain later confirmed by his physician. Under O.C.G.A. § 30-5-4(a), such conduct meets the legal threshold for elder abuse and intentional infliction of emotional distress: deliberate action, outrageous behavior, causation, and demonstrable injury.

This was not bureaucratic error; it was design—intimidation dressed in procedure, an abuse of power meant to preserve a narrative long discredited. The ghost of Russiagate lingered, haunting agencies unwilling to confess their failure. These were not compliance checks but intelligence operations, calibrated to unsettle pastors, distort truth into suspicion, and turn faith into evidence.

When my father was imprisoned in the Soviet Union, his interrogators called him an "enemy of the people." Forty years later, in the land that promised freedom, his American counterparts called him a "person of interest." The vocabulary had changed, but the spirit remained. And because he would not yield, his son became the next target.

Our stories were decades apart but written by the same Author. That truth —etched across two lifetimes—has not changed. It deepens with every trial, confirming that the same God who governs history still vindicates His own.

For in every generation, truth stands trial before power. Laws may bend, and courts may falter, but justice is never extinguished—it only waits to be recognized. My parents' Soviet accusers once called them enemies of the state; their American interrogators now call them persons of interest. Yet in both eras, the verdict that matters most has already been rendered by a higher court. What men twist for accusation, God redeems for testimony. And though lies may echo for a season, they cannot outlast the voice of truth—for the Author of this story still holds the final word.

Arbitrary by Design

What DHS and USCIS did not adequately account for is that my parents' ministry did not operate in isolation. Like all ministries, it existed within the constraints of real-world events—some of which no individual, organization, or government could control. Within a short span of time, two such events occurred, each widely recognized in both theological and legal contexts as extraordinary and unforeseeable: a global pandemic and a major armed conflict in Eastern Europe.

First came COVID-19.

International borders closed. Commercial air travel halted. Churches suspended in-person services. Conferences and mission gatherings were canceled worldwide. Ministries dependent on international travel and personal presence were disrupted across the board, often indefinitely. These interruptions were not discretionary choices or signs of abandonment; they were universal limitations imposed by a global public health emergency.

Then came war.

Russia's military action in Ukraine fractured long-standing relationships, disrupted religious initiatives, and severed channels of cooperation that had taken decades to establish. Sanctions were imposed, visas were revoked, and international travel became impracticable or impossible. Ministries with ties to the region were compelled to pause or restructure their work—not because of misconduct, but because the external environment rendered ordinary operations unworkable.

Despite the scope and severity of these events, DHS and USCIS adjudicators treated the resulting disruptions not as extraordinary circumstances affecting ministries worldwide, but as potential indicators of inconsistency or concern. Long-recognized legal principles governing force majeure, impossibility, and changed circumstances were not meaningfully reflected in the adjudicative analysis.

Under the Administrative Procedure Act, agency action is unlawful when it is "arbitrary, capricious, an abuse of discretion, or otherwise not in accordance with law."[1] An agency acts arbitrarily when it fails to consider relevant factors, ignores obvious external constraints, or draws adverse inferences unsupported by the record. Here, globally documented events—pandemic-related shutdowns and an active war—were treated as if they were discretionary anomalies rather than unavoidable realities.

This omission had material consequences.

Rather than resolving my parents' petitions based on the totality of circumstances, their cases remained pending for extended periods while additional inquiries were conducted. Administrative delays accumulated. Routine interviews expanded in scope and duration. Standard adjudicative timelines were repeatedly extended without clear explanation or resolution.

Over time, the focus appeared to shift away from statutory eligibility and toward open-ended inquiry. Yet no evidence of wrongdoing, improper influence, or disqualifying conduct was ever produced.

The inquiries yielded no adverse findings.

Nevertheless, the prolonged process itself imposed significant burdens. Years of unresolved status limited my parents' ability to plan, travel, and continue ministry activities. Their legal position was not resolved through a definitive adjudication, but rather eroded through delay. The absence of a final determination effectively functioned as a denial without the procedural clarity that ordinarily accompanies one.

For those who have lived under systems where administrative delay substitutes for formal action, this pattern is familiar. When decisive judgment is withheld, uncertainty itself becomes consequential. When cases remain unresolved indefinitely, the practical effect can mirror adverse action without the safeguards of transparency or finality.

Scripture names this quiet injustice with restraint:
"Justice is turned back, and righteousness stands far away; for truth has stumbled in the public squares" (Isaiah 59:14, ESV).

My parents had encountered similar dynamics before.

Under Soviet rule, religious life was often constrained not through immediate prosecution, but through prolonged monitoring, restriction, and administrative pressure. While the systems differ, the effect—constraint through process rather than verdict—bears resemblance.

America promised something different.

Yet here, too, faith carried a cost—paid not through criminal sanction, but through extended uncertainty, lost years, and the erosion of legal security. This was not the result of a single adverse decision, but of a process that never reached one.

---

[1] Administrative Procedure Act, 5 U.S.C. § 706(2)(A).

In the end, the system achieved a familiar outcome without issuing a verdict: faith endured, but lives were disrupted; status was diminished without formal adjudication.

Part III

America the Way It Is Not Supposed to Be

PART III

There was a time—not so long ago—when the world looked upon America with a kind of reverent wonder. Not because she was perfect, but because she aspired to be good. She was a place where families could grow roots, where neighbors lifted one another, where justice felt attainable because truth still meant something. The promise of liberty was never merely a line etched in stone; it was a lived invitation. Hope breathed in her streets.

But today, that goodness feels fragile—thin enough to tear, almost as though it has already slipped away.

Across the nation, families fracture under economic strain they never expected to face. Communities divide not only by ideology, but by suspicion. Neighbors study each other with narrowed eyes, unsure whom to trust, unsure which headlines to believe. Anger hums beneath the surface of national life, and fear has seeped deep into the American soul. The nation that once welcomed the tired, the poor, and the huddled masses now trembles at the sight of strangers—and too often at the sight of one another.

Scripture calls people to a different way: *"You shall love your neighbor as yourself"* (Mark 12:31). Yet in the public square, Americans do not merely disagree; they demonize. They speak as though ideological opponents are enemies rather than neighbors. They forget that *"the anger of man does not produce the righteousness of God"* (James 1:20). And the fruit of this forgetting is bitter—visible from the family dinner table to the halls of Congress.

America remains powerful. But increasingly, she is no longer well.

A Nation Losing Its Way

Across cities and towns, scenes unfold that would have once been unthinkable—scenes more fitting for a distant authoritarian regime than for the land of the free. In neighborhoods where children ride bicycles and families grill on porches, masked, unidentifiable, heavily armed individuals now roam in camo, olive, or tactical brown. They emerge from unmarked SUVs with rifles strapped across their chests. They move not like officers of the law, but like occupiers.

They introduce themselves to no one. They show no badges. They name no agency they represent.

This is not the calm professionalism that real policing demands. It is theater—militarized, anonymous, and dangerous.

Many who join these tactical units do so not out of a calling to serve but for the financial incentives, the bonuses, or the rush that unrestrained force provides. Others join because they could not meet the standards of genuine policing—too impulsive, too unstable, or too enamored with power to operate within the bounds of constitutional duty. A real badge demands accountability; anonymity requires none. The very restraints that make policing honorable are the ones these masked actors avoid.

America as It Is

They stalk residential streets. They peer into windows. They trail workers on their way to jobs that already strain their bodies and their spirits. They seize men and women outside churches, grocery stores, factories, and schools—often without warrants, often without explanation. Videos circulate of parents forced to the ground, restrained, and pushed into vehicles that vanish around corners while crying children stand frozen in disbelief, crying for a mother or father who moments earlier stood beside them.

This is not policing.
This is not safety.
This is the quiet rise of America's anonymous enforcers—unregulated, unaccountable, and concealed behind masks.

And perhaps most sobering: this is not the America people believed in.

A Moral Crisis, Not a Political One

America's crisis runs deeper than politics. It is spiritual—a wound in the national conscience.

Policy failures alone cannot explain what is happening. What Americans face today is a loss of compassion, a diminishing sense of human dignity. The nation has forgotten what Scripture declares plainly: *"Do not neglect to show hospitality to strangers, for thereby some have entertained angels unawares"* (Hebrews 13:2).

Instead of hospitality, America offers suspicion.
Instead of welcome, she offers fear.
Instead of justice, she offers bureaucracy wrapped in the language of righteousness.

Immigrants—many fleeing violence, persecution, or poverty—are treated not as neighbors but as threats. They labor in fields, restaurants, warehouses, and hospitals. They build homes they will never own. They care for children and elderly parents. They pay taxes, contribute to their communities, and live quietly, often invisibly.

And yet they are hunted with a zeal that should be reserved for actual threats to the nation.

It is easier to chase the harmless than to confront the harmful.
It is easier to overpower the weak than to restrain the strong.

This moral inversion is more than a policy misstep—it is a revelation of national character. It reveals what America has become and warns what she may yet become more fully.

The Hypocrisy of Compassion

America often proclaims itself the defender of religious liberty around the world. Politicians deliver speeches condemning the persecution of Christians in Nigeria, North Korea, or Iran. Churches raise funds, advocacy groups issue statements, and diplomats promise action to "protect the persecuted." Yet while voices in Washington decry the imprisonment of believers overseas, agents on American soil round up those same believers when they seek refuge here.

Claiming to care for Christians in Nigeria while detaining, deporting, and confining them in for-profit detention centers on U.S. soil is moral schizophrenia—a form of national cognitive dissonance that cannot stand before either God or truth. How can a nation claim to defend religious freedom abroad while violating it at home? How can it condemn persecution in one land while facilitating it in another, hidden beneath the language of policy and procedure?

Many of those detained in the United States fled nations where following Christ meant imprisonment, torture, or death. They came believing that America was a place where faith was free, where worship was protected, and where conscience would not be punished. Yet here they find themselves stripped of dignity, locked in facilities that function as modern-day concentration camps—confined, coerced into labor, and silenced once again.

Can a Christian who escaped persecution in Nigeria or China freely practice his or her faith while being held in a detention cell in Georgia or Arizona? Can believers gather for worship when every movement is monitored and every prayer gathering treated with suspicion? What kind of freedom is this, when the same hand that waves the flag of liberty abroad signs the orders that chain believers at home?

There is a profound moral dissonance in a government that funds international campaigns for "religious liberty" while permitting federal agencies to persecute the faithful within its own borders. True justice is not selective; true compassion is not partisan. To defend persecuted Christians abroad while detaining them here is to trade truth for optics, and conscience for convenience.

The hypocrisy runs deeper still. The same churches that sponsor missions to the persecuted abroad often remain silent when those same believers are caged within a few miles of their own sanctuaries. It is easier to send aid across an ocean than to confront injustice across town. It is safer to pray for persecuted believers in foreign lands than to stand beside them when they are handcuffed on American streets.

Religious liberty cannot survive as an export if it is not preserved as a domestic reality. If America continues to preach freedom while practicing captivity, it will soon find that its moral authority has collapsed entirely. For in God's eyes, there is no distinction between the Nigerian Christian imprisoned for his faith and the Nigerian believer detained in an America for seeking refuge. Both cry out to the same Lord of justice—and both are heard.

"Woe to you, scribes and Pharisees, hypocrites! For you travel across sea and land to make a single proselyte, and when he becomes a proselyte, you make him twice as much a child of hell as yourselves." (Matthew 23:15)

When faith becomes a banner rather than a burden, and compassion becomes a slogan rather than a sacrifice, the Church itself risks joining the ranks of those Christ once condemned: defenders of religion, but enemies of truth.

The Strangers Among You

When the Scriptures speak about the foreigner, they do not describe him as a threat or a criminal, but as one who deserves justice, dignity, and love. The Lord told His people, "You shall treat the stranger who sojourns with you as the native among you, and you shall love him as yourself, for you were strangers in the land of Egypt" (Leviticus 19:34). In God's eyes, the immigrant is not an outsider to be feared but a neighbor to be embraced.

Yet in America today, media narratives and certain politicians describe immigration as a "national emergency" and an "invasion." Migrants are often labeled "military-age men," as though their presence signifies a coming war. But this language distorts reality. These are not soldiers arriving with weapons; they are workers arriving with empty hands—ready to labor, ready to build, ready to provide. They are not "military-age" but "working age." When America invades, it does so with bombs and fire. When America is supposedly "invaded," it is by men and women willing to clean homes, harvest fields, and pour concrete—all in hope of feeding their families.

What many in the Department of Homeland Security, the FBI, and similar agencies fail to recognize is that their tactics do more than enforce policy—they intrude upon sacred ground. Their raids, interrogations, and surveillance disrupt religious freedom and violate the confidential bonds between pastors and those they shepherd. Houses of worship—churches and para-church ministries—were meant to be sanctuaries, protected from intrusion unless a lawful, judicial warrant requires otherwise. Yet far too often, the force of the state is not aimed at criminal networks or violent offenders, but at unarmed individuals who do not speak English, do not know their rights, and do not have the power to defend themselves. The vulnerable become the target, while the truly dangerous go untouched.

Immigrants are not the destroyers of the American way of life. They are, in fact, the backbone of its comfort and prosperity. They pick the crops that feed families, clean the spaces where others live and work, and build the houses and roads that sustain communities. They take on work that is physically demanding, often dangerous, and almost always overlooked—the work most Americans cannot or will not do. In truth, many employers would never consider hiring fellow Americans for such tasks because the cost would be far too high.

This reality should humble the nation. Immigrants labor quietly, often unseen, making possible the very conveniences and comforts others take for granted. Instead of condemnation, they deserve gratitude. Instead of suspicion, they deserve hospitality. For in serving them, Americans serve Christ Himself, who said, "I was a stranger and you welcomed Me" (Matthew 25:35).

The U.S. government and its agencies, however, are often complicit in the opposite. Families are torn apart; individuals are uprooted and shuffled from detention center to detention center—many of which are operated by for-profit, publicly traded institutions. In these facilities, detainees are frequently forced to work for two to four dollars per day, barely enough to afford the most basic necessities. This is coerced labor under the guise of policy, mirroring the very exploitation condemned by the law.

Filling private detention centers and holding people for as long as possible is the American iteration of government-run, taxpayer-funded human trafficking. It is not about deportation—it is about profit. The system exists to extract as many taxpayer dollars as possible while keeping human beings locked away in the murky gray haze of immigration law.

This is not accidental—it is structural. The incentive is not to resolve cases quickly but to prolong detention, extracting maximum financial return from every person held. It is not merely unjust—it is predatory.

And it is bipartisan.

Neither political party meaningfully solves immigration. Both instead perpetuate the crisis because the continued presence, visibility, and suffering of undocumented people serves political ends. For one side, detainees become proof of "enforcement." For the other, they become symbols of "compassion" and outrage. In both cases, human beings are rendered instrumental—kept in limbo not because the law requires it, but because unresolved bodies generate donations, votes, headlines, and platforms.

Exploiting the Stranger

Under the Trafficking Victims Protection Act (TVPA), 22 U.S.C. § 7102(11), human trafficking is defined as the recruitment, harboring, transportation, provision, or obtaining of a person for labor or services through the use of force, fraud, or coercion for the purpose of involuntary servitude, debt bondage, or slavery; or for a commercial sex act induced by force, fraud, or coercion. In plain terms, human trafficking is the exploitation of people through force, fraud, or coercion for another's benefit.

Crucially, "services" under the TVPA is not limited to traditional labor. It encompasses any compelled action, availability, or benefit a person is forced to provide for another—whether physical, emotional, psychological, domestic, or relational—when obtained through force, fraud, or coercion. Availability itself can constitute a service when a person is intentionally confined, displayed, or maintained in a condition of dependence for institutional, financial, or political advantage.

Within immigration detention, these elements are tragically present. Facilities compel detainees into forced labor because no alternative exists. The system depends on the very people it confines to keep it running—cooking meals, washing laundry, cleaning floors, and performing manual labor and basic operations that facility staff cannot or will not do. What was supposed to be a temporary holding process becomes something far more troubling: a closed-loop system in which human beings become the machinery that sustains their own captivity.

Even when these facilities are at or beyond capacity, they still rely heavily on detainee labor simply to function. If detainees collectively refused to work, meals would not be prepared, laundry would not be washed, common areas would not be cleaned, and the system would grind to a halt within days. The power dynamic is unmistakable: detainees are coerced into working not through overt force but through deprivation—lack of alternatives, lack of freedom, and a structure that quietly punishes those who refuse.

This is not merely poor management; it is institutional exploitation, built into the very design of detention itself. People who should be protected under the law are instead reduced to a captive labor force with no choice but to maintain the very system that profits from keeping them locked inside.

This practice bears disturbing similarities to some of America's darkest precedents: the convict leasing systems of the late nineteenth and early twentieth centuries, in which prisoners were forced to work to generate revenue for states and private enterprises; the internment camps of World War II, where Japanese Americans were compelled to labor under confinement despite having committed no crime; and other moments when government blurred the line between justice and exploitation. These facilities may have different names today, but their function—to profit from prolonged human captivity—echoes those historical abuses.

But the exploitation does not stop at physical labor. Detainees are also compelled to *remain available*—as bodies to fill beds, justify budgets, support contracts, sustain political narratives, and prolong a manufactured crisis. They are warehoused not because resolution is impossible, but because resolution would collapse the very structures that profit—financially and politically—from their confinement.

This is exploitation of the stranger, refined for modern America: legalized, outsourced, rhetorically sanitized, and defended by both parties—yet bearing all the essential marks of trafficking as defined by the law itself.

According to TRAC data from April 2025, forty-five of the 181 ICE detention facilities were operating above capacity—many of them run by the nation's largest private prison contractors.[2] A recent Government Accountability Office report concluded that the Department of Homeland Security's inspection programs lack clear performance goals and measurable oversight, leaving violations uncorrected for years.[3] Unannounced inspections by the Office of Inspector General have repeatedly found ICE failing to meet standards for medical care, environmental health, grievance processes, and basic staff–detainee communication.[4]

Beyond the statistics, this system devastates families. Children are left without parents, spouses without partners, and entire communities without breadwinners and leaders. The fear that follows an arrest lingers long after the moment passes—families live in constant vigilance, afraid to answer the door, afraid to drive to work or school, afraid that the next knock means another loved one will disappear. This is not simply a legal process; it is a trauma machine that grinds down families emotionally, spiritually, and financially.

The true punishment is not deportation itself—it is the slow, grinding process that leads to it. Deportations often take months, sometimes years, while people are held in facilities that are overcrowded, privately operated, and chronically failing to meet even the most basic health, hygiene, and due process standards. These places do not function as waystations; they function as cages—twenty-first-century, for-profit concentration camps. The government has outsourced human detention to corporations whose profit model depends on keeping people locked up for as long as possible.

This is not justice; it is punishment without trial. It conflates enforcement with retribution and undermines the principles the United States claims to uphold: due process, human dignity, and equal protection under the law. A government that detains indiscriminately—for profit and without regard to legal status—betrays its founding values.

Congress and the administration must end the use of prolonged, for-profit detention as the default mechanism of immigration enforcement. Alternatives exist—supervised release, rapid adjudication, and community monitoring—that are humane, effective, and far less costly to the taxpayer. What is required is leadership willing to ensure that immigration enforcement aligns with constitutional principles and that the United States never again repeats the errors of its past.

---

[2] Transactional Records Access Clearinghouse (TRAC), "ICE Detention: April 2025 Data," Syracuse University, April 2025, https://trac.syr.edu/immigration/detention.

[3] U.S. Government Accountability Office, Immigration Detention: DHS Needs to Improve Oversight of Facility Conditions, GAO-25-107580 (Washington, DC: GAO, 2025).

[4] U.S. Department of Homeland Security, Office of Inspector General, ICE's Inspections and Monitoring of Detention Facilities Do Not Lead to Sustained Compliance

The result is a detention system that no longer resembles justice. Instead, it functions as a taxpayer-funded machine for indefinite imprisonment and coerced labor—one that punishes asylum seekers, individuals with pending cases, and those in tenuous legal limbo no differently than people with criminal convictions or repeated unlawful entries. The system is so dysfunctional that it often ensnares even those who should never be subject to it at all—lawful visa holders, permanent residents, and, at times, even U.S. citizens—treating them as though they were criminals.

This is not an immigration system; it is an incarceration industry. And most alarming of all, it treats everyone the same. Those who entered legally, visa holders, and even individuals with pending applications or clean criminal records are lumped together with those who have serious convictions or repeated unlawful entries. Constitutional protections—liberty, presumption of innocence, and the right to timely adjudication—are trampled in the name of "processing."

This is not merely a policy failure; it is an assault on the very principles America claims to defend. History offers a chilling parallel. During World War II, Japanese Americans—citizens and lawful residents—were forcibly uprooted and confined to internment camps without charges or trials. The government later confessed its wrongdoing and offered an apology. Yet today, detention-first enforcement echoes that same spirit of collective punishment: people are not confronted for what they have done, but for who they are, where they come from, or simply because they are caught in the gears of a broken system.

And the tragedy is this: America has seen these shadows before. The nation has lived through moments when fear overpowered truth, when suspicion replaced justice, and when the Constitution—so boldly proclaimed—fell silent in the very hour it was most needed.

Old Ghosts

The specter of McCarthyism still lingers—when suspicion alone was enough to ruin lives and careers. In our own day, suspicion alone is enough to justify shackles, detention, and months or years of uncertainty.

This is punishment without trial. It conflates enforcement with retribution, eroding the principles of due process, human dignity, and equal protection under the law. A nation that detains indiscriminately, for profit, betrays its own founding ideals.

Congress and the administration must act. Prolonged, for-profit detention cannot remain the default tool of immigration enforcement. Humane and effective alternatives exist—supervised release, community monitoring, and accelerated adjudication—all far less expensive to the taxpayer and far more consistent with constitutional principles.

PART III

America must choose whether it will continue to run a shadow system of detention camps or return to the principles of liberty and justice that made it the nation so many risk their lives to reach.

America's Immigration Legacy

The history of American immigration law tells a sobering story. From the very beginning, the nation's approach to immigration has been a blend of welcome and exclusion, generosity and control—but always with power and profit close at hand. The first Naturalization Act of 1790 set the rules for who could belong, but only for "free white persons." Nearly a century later, the Immigration Act of 1882 introduced federal immigration control and imposed a head tax on every immigrant—a revenue stream drawn from those seeking refuge and opportunity.

Throughout the twentieth century, Congress repeatedly rewrote the rules. The Immigration and Nationality Act of 1965 eliminated the openly discriminatory quota system and replaced it with family- and skills-based preferences. Two decades later, the Immigration Reform and Control Act of 1986 added employer sanctions and a legalization program—but it also entrenched a system that left millions vulnerable and easily exploited. The last major overhaul in 1990 restructured immigration categories but failed to create a lasting path for the millions who remained in the shadows.

Meanwhile, a parallel system took shape—one that turned immigration enforcement into a business model. In 1983, Corrections Corporation of America (now CoreCivic) was founded, pioneering the concept of private, for-profit incarceration. By 2004, facilities like the Stewart Detention Center in Georgia were built specifically to house immigration detainees under government contract. With a capacity of nearly 1,900 people, Stewart became a warehouse for those whose status was unresolved—men and women held far from their families, often compelled to work for dollars a day to clean, cook, and operate the very facility that confined them.

This is not accidental—it is structural. The incentives are clear: prolong detention, maximize bed space, and extract labor at the lowest possible cost. The longer a person's case drags on, the more money flows to private contractors. The more fear is stoked about "illegal immigration," the more political capital can be gained by promising to be "tough," regardless of whether the policies address the underlying issues.

What America has built is a system that profits from human suffering. It draws money from taxpayers to fund detention centers, rewards corporations that incarcerate the vulnerable, and uses migrants as bargaining chips in political negotiations. This is not merely bad policy—it is a moral indictment. It reveals a legacy that has drifted far from biblical justice, a system that leverages the pain of the powerless for profit and political gain.

Biblical Commands

"Hear, O Israel: The Lord our God, the Lord is one. And you shall love the Lord your God with all your heart and with all your soul and with all your mind and with all your strength. ... You shall love your neighbor as yourself. There is no other commandment greater than these." (Mark 12:29–31)

Scripture leaves no room for ambiguity. The Lord commands His people, "Do no wrong or violence to the resident alien, the fatherless, and the widow, nor shed innocent blood in this place" (Jeremiah 22:3). He warns against exploiting the vulnerable for personal or political gain: "He executes justice for the fatherless and the widow, and loves the sojourner, giving him food and clothing" (Deuteronomy 10:18). "Cursed be anyone who perverts the justice due to the sojourner, the fatherless, and the widow. And all the people shall say, 'Amen'" (Deuteronomy 27:19). And again, "Love the sojourner, therefore, for you were sojourners in the land of Egypt" (Deuteronomy 10:19).

The Jews were once aliens. The Puritans who founded America were aliens. God's Word calls His people to defend the cause of the sojourner and the orphan, to refuse to oppress the stranger, and to remember that we ourselves were once aliens in need of mercy.

And yet today, in America, the Church remains silent.

And yet, despite the clarity of Scripture and the weight of God's commands, a chasm now stretches between what America professes and what America practices. The very passages Christians underline in their Bibles are ignored when the sojourner stands at their doorstep. The same hands raised in worship on Sunday often remain still when justice calls on Monday.

It is here—between God's revealed will and the nation's hardened habits —that the great tragedy emerges. For when a people who once knew compassion choose instead convenience, and when a Church entrusted with God's heart for the vulnerable chooses silence, what follows is not merely inconsistency. It is moral collapse.

A Moral Failure

Migrants are treated worse than animals. Shelter animals are fed, sheltered, and cared for, while men, women, and children are locked in detention centers under conditions that strip them of dignity and hope. These migrants are not defined by crime—they are human beings made in the image of God. Many labor simply to feed their children, to escape violence, or to contribute to the communities where they live. Even among those who have stumbled or been convicted, their worth does not vanish, nor does their dignity dissolve. The system paints them all with the same brush, but God sees them as souls in need of justice, mercy, and redemption.

To strip them of freedom, compel them to work for near-slavery wages, and use them as pawns in political games is a moral failure. It is a breach of both law and conscience—a denial of the biblical principles upon which a just society must stand.

America must face the truth: immigrants are not a curse but a blessing. They embody courage, perseverance, and sacrifice. Their presence enriches neighborhoods, strengthens the economy, and reflects the diverse tapestry that points toward God's kingdom, where people from "every tribe and language and people and nation" gather before the throne (Revelation 5:9). Welcoming the stranger is not merely a matter of public policy—it is an act of obedience to God's Word.

Instead of welcome, migrants are hunted down. Many came fleeing death threats, persecution, and war, yet they are pursued across the country as though they were prey. Those who chase them boast as if it were sport, delighting in the power they have been given. Families are torn apart, children are ripped from their parents—and still, the Church remains silent.

This silence is not without reason. Such policies allow even the smallest, most insecure citizen to feel superior to someone. They create a counterfeit sense of strength, convincing people that humiliating the powerless proves national might. It is always easier to beat down the weak than to confront true evil. It is always easier to dress in tactical gear, hide behind a mask, and chase the unarmed than to face a real adversary. When it is three, four, five, or six against one—what is it but a hunt?

But what then? If every "illegal immigrant" were driven out, who would wash dishes in restaurants, build and paint the houses, clean them, or harvest the fields? America depends on the very people it despises. Their labor sustains the nation's comforts, its conveniences, and its daily life.

A Nation of Immigrants

America has forgotten that it is a nation of immigrants. With the exception of its Native peoples, every family line traces back to another land. From the beginning, immigrants have been central to the nation's story—shaping its culture, building its institutions, and sustaining its strength. Some of the highest leaders remind the nation of this truth: Vice President Kamala Harris is the daughter of immigrants; President Barack Obama's father came from Kenya; President Donald Trump's mother was born in Scotland; President Andrew Jackson was the son of Irish immigrants. Senator Marco Rubio is the son of Cuban immigrants, and First Lady Melania Trump is herself an immigrant. Even those whose families came generations earlier—like Presidents Woodrow Wilson, James Buchanan, and Herbert Hoover—were shaped by immigrant roots. To forget this heritage is to forget what it means to be American.

America as It Is

Scripture calls God's people to remember this truth: "You shall treat the stranger who sojourns with you as the native among you, and you shall love him as yourself, for you were strangers in the land of Egypt: I am the LORD your God" (Leviticus 19:34). And again, "Do not neglect to show hospitality to strangers, for thereby some have entertained angels unawares" (Hebrews 13:2). If America is to live faithfully, it must not despise the immigrant but honor the image of God in every person.

When a nation remembers that its people were once strangers, compassion naturally follows. But when that memory fades, the heart grows cold, and the stranger becomes an enemy. America stands at such a crossroads now—between remembrance and forgetting, between mercy and fear. And history is not silent about what happens when a nation chooses the wrong path.

Lessons of History

History warns where this path leads. The treatment of migrants today echoes the early years of Nazi Germany, when rights were stripped from those deemed undesirable, and many celebrated it as proof of national strength. Those steps paved the way for destruction. Migrants in America today are denied the very rights the Constitution claims to guarantee to all people—rights that, in truth, are not merely constitutional but God-given.

Migrants are no longer seen as human beings—not even as creatures worthy of care—but as blemishes to be erased from the nation's landscape. Yet in God's economy, they are like the living stones that hold up the house. They are the unseen hands doing the work that keeps the nation standing, the servants who fill the gaps others refuse to fill. Remove them, and the structure may appear spotless for a moment, but its foundation will begin to crack. Without their presence, America will not be purified—it will be hollowed out, weakened, and left to collapse under the weight of its own injustice and pride.

History invites every generation to decide whether it will walk toward light or drift back into darkness. And when compassion grows cold and fear becomes a teacher, the darkness begins to look familiar again—shaped by the same patterns of suspicion and cruelty that once scarred the world.

Familiar Darkness

In the heart of American cities, in broad daylight and before the eyes of ordinary citizens, scenes unfold that recall humanity's darkest memories. Men in light brown or green uniforms—masked, armed, and anonymous—seize people off sidewalks, from cars, workplaces, and bus stops. Families watch in terror as loved ones are forced into unmarked vehicles and driven away. No warrant. No notice. No explanation. And like the ghosts of another century, many simply disappear—vanished into a system that tells their families nothing.

These moments are recorded on cell phones and shared online, but the normalization of such images reveals a deeper decay. History has seen this before. Each time, it began the same way—with uniforms, silence, and the quiet consent of a frightened public.

The brownshirts of Nazi Germany once roamed the streets under the pretense of "restoring order." They broke into homes, rounded up citizens, and dragged them away while neighbors pretended not to see. Those taken often vanished without a word. No charges were filed, no families notified. Days later, officials would claim ignorance. Their uniforms became symbols of a state that could seize anyone at any time—and answer to no one.

The Gestapo perfected the same terror through bureaucracy. Their arrests were described as "protective custody," as though the victims were being safeguarded. Instead, they were made to disappear into a system of prisons and camps from which few ever returned. The Gestapo taught the world how terror hides best—under the language of legality.

In East Germany, the Stasi replaced open violence with psychological warfare. They could take a man from his home in the middle of the night, leaving no record of arrest, no information for his family. Or they could simply make him vanish socially—fired from his job, blacklisted, watched by his own neighbors. Surveillance became a substitute for shackles, but the effect was the same: silence through fear.

The Soviet KGB extended this pattern across continents. It called itself "the sword and shield" of the Communist Party, yet its true function was control through disappearance. Those who were taken—writers, pastors, dissenters—were erased from public life, their names whispered only in secret. Family members received no notice, no trial, no body. Only silence.

Even now, in Ukraine, videos show military recruiters dragging men off buses and sidewalks, forcing them into vans to fill quotas. Locals call them "people snatchers." Families learn of their fate days later, if at all. Authorities deny wrongdoing, calling each case "isolated." The denials echo the same hollow words once spoken by every regime that learned to disguise coercion as duty.

And now, in the United States, we witness a new form of this old horror. ICE agents—masked, armed, and dressed in shifting combinations of camo, light brown, or green—move through residential neighborhoods and city streets like an unmarked militia. They are not merely uniformed officers; they are *anonymous*. No name tags. No identifying numbers. No transparency. Every effort is made to conceal who they are and whom they answer to. America's new secret police are, quite literally, secret.

They seize men and women without judicial warrants, often in front of their children. They pull people from cars, workplaces, schools, even churches. The videos circulate online: human beings forced to the ground, handcuffed, and shoved into unmarked vans that speed away with no explanation. Families are left standing in driveways or on sidewalks, stunned and powerless, waiting for calls that may never come.

But the visible arrests are only part of the story. Across the country, ununiformed and anonymous agents in unmarked cars now stalk their targets in plain sight—circling apartment complexes, peering through windows, waiting outside homes and schools. They surveil families as if they were criminals, sometimes for days, until the moment of ambush arrives. Neighbors whisper, children hide, and ordinary life bends under the weight of fear. This is not policing; it is psychological warfare—designed to break resolve, to intimidate communities into silence, and to remind everyone who watches that power no longer answers to principle.

Those who vanish are not enemies of the state. Many have pending legal cases, work permits, or families who depend on them. Yet the system treats them as disposable, erasing them into bureaucratic limbo—sometimes for months, sometimes for years—without trial, without record, without the decency of notice.

The resemblance to the past is not rhetorical; it is real. The same elements are present: uniforms without names, power without oversight, and the ability to make human beings disappear without explanation. What once happened in the alleys of Berlin, the cellars of Lubyanka, or the prisons of East Germany now happens in parking lots and playgrounds across the American landscape—this time livestreamed to a public too distracted or desensitized to intervene.

When a government acquires the power to seize a person without cause, to hide them without trial, and to tell their families nothing, it has crossed the threshold that separates democracy from tyranny. And when a nation grows accustomed to such scenes—when fear becomes routine and silence becomes self-protection—it ceases to be free.

History does not repeat itself exactly; it rhymes with terrible precision. The same pattern unfolds: first justification, then normalization, and then the people begin to disappear.

America was meant to be different. It was founded on the belief that every person is endowed by God with dignity, due process, and freedom from arbitrary power. But when masked men can seize civilians in the open and vanish them into a system that profits from their captivity, then something sacred has been lost—not only in government, but in the nation's soul.

The Erosion of Restraint

In the American tradition, law enforcement was never meant to resemble an occupying army. The Founders understood that the power to police must always remain accountable to the people—not above them. That is why they enshrined in the Constitution the right to due process and habeas corpus: the guarantee that no person may be seized, detained, or imprisoned without lawful cause and judicial review. This principle is not a bureaucratic technicality; it is the line that separates a free nation from a police state.

Over time, however, that line has begun to blur. The rise of militarized policing—armored vehicles on residential streets, tactical gear in suburban neighborhoods, and the normalization of masked, heavily armed units—represents a dangerous shift in America's civic DNA. The Posse Comitatus Act of 1878 was meant to prevent precisely this: the use of the U.S. military in domestic law enforcement. While the Act limits federal troops, it allows exceptions when the National Guard is under the control of a state governor. But once "federalized" under the President's command, the Guard falls under the same prohibitions—at least in theory. In practice, the distinction has eroded. Federal agencies now operate with a level of militarization that effectively blurs the constitutional separation between the soldier and the peace officer.

True law enforcement does not wage war against the public; it protects those whom the Constitution protects. The mindset of militarized policing—"dominate, neutralize, eliminate"—belongs on foreign battlefields, not on American streets. Soldiers are trained to overwhelm and destroy an enemy. Police are meant to preserve life and restore order. These are opposite callings, requiring opposite mentalities. The transformation of the police uniform from blue to camo is more than aesthetic; it is symbolic of a nation forgetting that its guardians are not meant to be its conquerors.

Today, it is not uncommon to see "law enforcement" agents dressed in tactical assault gear—clad in olive, sand, or digital camouflage, faces hidden behind masks and visors. These are not the traditional blues of the community officer, visible and accountable; they are the colors of occupying forces. The sight of anonymous, heavily armed men patrolling American streets—sometimes without clear identification, sometimes in unmarked vehicles—should alarm every citizen who values liberty.

The danger is compounded by who fills these ranks. Many veterans of foreign wars are fast-tracked into law enforcement and ICE positions through veterans' preference programs, virtually guaranteeing them employment. Yet not all military experience is equal. Those who have seen combat or participated in occupations abroad carry instincts forged for warfare, not for community policing. Combat trauma and conditioning often persist for life. The habits necessary for survival in battle—suspicion, aggression, readiness to kill—are profoundly incompatible with the restraint, patience, and empathy required for civil duty.

For that reason, veterans who have served in combat zones should not automatically be funneled into domestic law enforcement. Exception, not entitlement, should be the rule. Those who once occupied foreign streets should not be given unchecked authority to patrol American ones. Soldiers are trained to attack with overwhelming force; police must be trained to de-escalate. The two mindsets cannot coexist without tragedy.

What many civilians fail to realize is this: the patterns learned abroad eventually return home. Years of conducting raids in foreign nations—with little accountability and even less transparency—shaped a culture of force that has now migrated onto American soil. What was normalized "over there" has quietly become acceptable "right here," and the line between foreign operations and domestic policing has nearly disappeared.

What is unfolding is not "public safety"—it is militarized theater, and it is dangerous. Masked, unidentifiable, heavily armed individuals now roam American streets under the guise of "law enforcement," though many bear little resemblance to genuine officers. Some join for money and bonuses; others are drawn precisely because their force and authority go unchecked. Many could never meet the standards of real policing—too unstable, too impulsive, or too enamored with power to function under the restraint and accountability true officers embrace.

They operate from unmarked vehicles, stalking neighborhoods, surveilling homes, peering through windows, and instilling fear in communities that once trusted their police. Real police identify themselves; occupiers hide their names. Real peacekeepers calm a situation; these agents inflame it.

This is not law enforcement. It is intimidation masquerading as authority.

This is not the America the Constitution envisioned. It is a slow-motion coup against the rule of law—an erosion of restraint disguised as "security." It is the normalization of the abnormal, the militarization of the mundane. Ironically, many who protested the so-called "new normal" during the COVID era now seem indifferent to the true "new normal": a culture of surveillance, censorship, and militarized policing that treats residents as suspects or enemies.

For the non-Christian, the Constitution serves as the ultimate moral compass of the republic—the supreme law of the land. It is not subordinate to the impulses of bureaucrats, the moods of the executive branch, or the shifting tides of popular opinion. Outside of a constitutional amendment, no politician's feelings or voters' fears can supersede it. The law exists precisely to protect the nation from the stupidity of the moment and the folly of the mob.

When masked men can detain civilians without warrants, when armored vehicles roll through peaceful neighborhoods, and when those sworn to protect begin to treat the governed as the enemy, the spirit of liberty has already begun to die. America does not need more weapons on its streets; it needs more wisdom in its institutions—and more courage in its people to declare that this must not become the norm.

PART III

History's Warning Signs

Every generation believes its crises are unique, yet history repeats the same warnings in different uniforms. America has seen this pattern before—moments when fear, ideology, or convenience led the state to turn its power against its own people. Each time, the promise of liberty was weakened, and each time, it was justified "for public safety."

After World War I, the Red Scare turned suspicion into policy. Ordinary workers, immigrants, and intellectuals were dragged from their homes in the Palmer Raids, accused of being communists or anarchists. Warrants were ignored, habeas corpus was suspended, and thousands were detained without cause. The justification was national security; the reality was state paranoia.

During the civil rights movement, COINTELPRO—the FBI's counterintelligence program—infiltrated churches, spied on pastors, and spread lies about peaceful reformers. The government, sworn to defend the Constitution, instead targeted those demanding that it be honored. And in 1970, at Kent State University, National Guardsmen opened fire on unarmed students protesting the Vietnam War, killing four and wounding nine. Fear and force replaced dialogue and restraint.

In every case, the same pattern emerged: fear created permission, permission bred excess, and excess birthed tragedy. And afterward—when the damage was done—the nation looked back in shame, promising it would never happen again.

Yet here we are again—unmarked vehicles, masked men, and militarized "task forces" detaining residents on American streets. The uniforms are different, the language is modern, but the principle is the same. History's cycle of repression repeats itself under new names and acronyms.

When a government forgets that its weapons exist to defend liberty, not to enforce compliance, it begins to resemble the very regimes it once condemned. The erosion of civil restraint never begins with a declaration—it begins with an exception, a justification, a single unchecked act of force. Soon, those exceptions become policy.

If America forgets her own history, she will relive it. The Constitution is not self-enforcing; it depends on citizens who remember why it was written. The same courage that once defied tyrants abroad must now be summoned to confront tyranny at home.

For no empire ever admits that it has become one. It only tells its citizens that the tanks in their streets, the masks on their police, and the surveillance in their homes are there "for their protection." But history whispers otherwise—and freedom, if it is to survive, demands that we listen.

America as It Is

The Worship of Power

History's warnings are mirrored in Scripture. No nation collapses without first corrupting its conscience. The prophets of old spoke not only to Israel and Judah but to every empire that exalts might over mercy and confuses fear with strength.

Assyria, the ancient superpower of its time, believed its military victories were proof of divine favor. Its armies crushed nations, paraded captives, and gloried in cruelty. Yet God declared through Isaiah:

"Woe to Assyria, the rod of My anger;
 the staff in their hands is My fury! ...
But he does not so intend,
 and his heart does not so think;
but it is in his heart to destroy,
 and to cut off nations not a few."
(Isaiah 10:5, 7)

Assyria's downfall came not from external invasion alone but from the rot of pride within. When power becomes its own justification, judgment is only a matter of time.

Babylon followed the same path. The prophet Habakkuk cried out, "The law is paralyzed, and justice never goes forth" (Habakkuk 1:4). Babylon worshiped conquest and control; it measured its greatness by its ability to subdue others. God answered that arrogance with a chilling decree:

"Because you have plundered many nations,
all the remnant of the peoples shall plunder you." (Habakkuk 2:8)

When law is paralyzed, when the guardians of justice become its violators, and when the oppressed cry out unheard, judgment does not delay forever.

Rome, too, built its glory on the promise of order through force—the *Pax Romana*, peace by domination. The same empire that crucified Christ prided itself on civilization while nailing the innocent to crosses. Rome's might could subdue the world, but it could not cleanse its own soul. Its roads carried both apostles and executioners; its laws protected the powerful and crushed the poor. In time, the empire that could conquer nations could no longer govern itself.

America now walks the same perilous road. It boasts of liberty but celebrates violence. It quotes Scripture at rallies but silences prophets who call for justice. It arms itself to the teeth and calls it peace; it cages the stranger and calls it security. It confuses moral courage with political power and worships the state as though it were God's chosen instrument of redemption.

The militarization of police, the surveillance of citizens, and the erosion of due process are not merely political issues—they are spiritual ones. They reveal what a nation truly believes about power, about human worth, and about the meaning of justice. When a government's tools begin to resemble the idols of Babylon more than the instruments of liberty, it has already begun to fall.

Scripture does not record the fall of these nations to satisfy curiosity; it records them to warn us: "Righteousness exalts a nation, but sin is a reproach to any people" (Proverbs 14:34). The pattern never changes: when nations reject truth, they invite tyranny. When they trade justice for control, they lose both.

Justice Unremembered

Scripture warns that when a nation's laws become weapons instead of safeguards, judgment is not far behind. God has never turned a blind eye to those who exploit the weak under the pretense of order or profit. "Woe to those who decree iniquitous decrees, and the writers who keep writing oppression," said Isaiah, "to turn aside the needy from justice and to rob the poor of My people of their right" (Isaiah 10:1–2).

These words were not written for ancient Israel alone. They echo across the centuries to every nation that claims righteousness while practicing injustice. When governments cloak cruelty in procedure and justify violence as policy, they repeat the very sins that once brought empires to ruin.

Amos warned of a people who "turn justice to wormwood and cast down righteousness to the earth" (Amos 5:7). He spoke to those who trampled the poor in their courts, who "afflict the righteous, take a bribe, and turn aside the needy in the gate" (Amos 5:12). Such words describe more than ancient corruption—they mirror our own age, where the powerless are detained, silenced, or erased while the powerful hide behind the machinery of law.

Through Jeremiah, God declared His standard with unflinching clarity:

"Do no wrong or violence to the resident alien, the fatherless, and the widow, nor shed innocent blood in this place." (Jeremiah 22:3)

This is not a suggestion; it is a divine command. And when nations ignore it, the consequences are inevitable. History testifies that injustice cannot be sustained indefinitely. It corrodes the conscience of a people and provokes the judgment of God.

The prophets spoke not only of judgment but of blindness—a moral blindness that spreads when comfort dulls conviction. "They have healed the wound of My people lightly, saying, 'Peace, peace,' when there is no peace" (Jeremiah 6:14). So too in our day, many soothe their conscience with slogans of security and legality while ignoring the pain of those taken, detained, and forgotten.

But God sees what man refuses to see. He hears the cries that never reach a courtroom. He remembers the names of those who vanish without trace. The widow, the fatherless, and the stranger still matter to Him, even when they no longer matter to the state.

A nation that forgets this truth invites its own undoing. The same God who once humbled Babylon, who judged Edom, Moab, and Israel for their oppression, remains sovereign still. His standard has not changed: "Let justice roll down like waters, and righteousness like an ever-flowing stream" (Amos 5:24).

The question is whether America will remember that righteousness exalts a nation—or whether it will continue down the path of those who learned too late that no empire is strong enough to outlast the justice of God.

A Nation Drifting from Its Soul

America was born from the conviction that freedom is sacred—that no man should bow to another except in reverence to God. Its founding words proclaimed that all people are "endowed by their Creator with certain unalienable Rights." Its Constitution enshrined limits on power so that no ruler could again play the tyrant. For a time, those ideals stood as a moral lighthouse to the world: liberty under law, order under conscience, government under God.

But a nation's words mean nothing when its deeds betray them. Today, the same republic that once declared independence from tyranny now uses its strength to impose it—not abroad, but at home. Federal agents in masks, armored police on city streets, government surveillance of citizens, and raids on places of worship: these are not symbols of freedom. They are the rituals of empire—the signs of a nation that has forgotten its own creed.

The words *We the People* have been quietly replaced by *Trust the System*. The Constitution, once revered as the guardian of liberty, is now treated as an inconvenience to be reinterpreted, bypassed, or ignored. The Bill of Rights, drafted to protect citizens from government overreach, is now routinely suspended in the name of "safety," "security," or "national interest."

America has become a land of moral inversion. It sends aid to persecuted Christians in Nigeria while arresting believers here for overstaying visas. It speaks of religious liberty while raiding churches under suspicion of "harboring" immigrants. It quotes Scripture on campaign stages, yet closes its borders to those who resemble the very people Christ commanded us to love. The contradiction is staggering. The cognitive dissonance is national policy.

The prophets once warned Israel that hypocrisy would bring ruin:

"This people draw near with their mouth and honor Me with their lips, while their hearts are far from Me." (Isaiah 29:13)

PART III

America now stands in that same place—lips full of praise, hands full of blood. It builds sanctuaries with one hand and detention centers with the other. It claims to defend freedom abroad while dismantling it at home. It lifts up the flag but tramples the conscience.
And yet, the Lord still pleads:

"If you amend your ways and your deeds,
    if you truly execute justice one with another,
if you do not oppress the sojourner, the fatherless, or the widow,
    then I will let you dwell in this place."
(Jeremiah 7:5–7)

This is not a political question—it is a moral reckoning. A nation cannot remain free while teaching its agents to act as occupiers. It cannot preserve liberty while normalizing deception, secrecy, and unaccountable force. The Constitution may define the structure of government, but only righteousness preserves its spirit.

America has been blessed more than any empire in history—but blessing without repentance becomes judgment. Power without humility becomes idolatry. And when a people no longer blush at injustice, they are already enslaved in spirit.

A Nation Governed by Fear

America's founders envisioned a nation restrained by law, not driven by fear. The Constitution was written precisely so that no government official—no matter how armed, how masked, or how emboldened—could wield power unchecked. The Bill of Rights was designed to protect individuals from the very abuses now recurring on American soil: warrantless searches, unreasonable seizures, and the arbitrary deprivation of liberty.

Yet today, families watch loved ones taken away without notice or explanation. Some disappear into detention systems for months, even years. Phone calls go unanswered. Court dates are delayed. Records are lost. Accountability dissolves into silence. It is not unlike what dark regimes once engineered—when those with power could make a person vanish, and those left behind were told nothing.

This is America the way it was not supposed to be.

It is the echo of a world we promised never to repeat—the world where force is easier than justice, where the vulnerable are preyed upon because they are powerless to resist, and where institutions serve themselves instead of the people they were made to protect.

It is a tragedy that in America, the land that proclaims liberty, so many now live with the quiet dread that the knock on the door may not be a neighbor…but someone wearing a mask.

A Call Not to Despair but to Discern

And yet—even now—hope is not lost.

Scripture assures God's people that "the light shines in the darkness, and the darkness has not overcome it" (John 1:5). The failures of a nation do not nullify the sovereignty of God. Brokenness does not cancel the possibility of redemption. America's story is not finished, and its destiny need not be written by fear.

There remains a path back—a road marked by repentance, humility, and courage.

For America's hope is not found in political platforms, military might, or masked enforcers patrolling the streets. Its hope is found in moral clarity, in the rediscovery of compassion, and in the courage to do justice, love mercy, and walk humbly with God. It is found in leaders who remember that power is stewardship, not entitlement, and in citizens who remember that the stranger, the worker, the immigrant, and the neighbor all bear the image of God.

A Nation Worth Saving

America is worth mourning because it is worth saving. The distance between what the nation is and what it was meant to be is vast, but it is not unbridgeable. It is bridged one act of truth at a time, one act of mercy at a time, one act of courage at a time.

The Church must rise again as a voice of conscience—not for one party or another, but for the Kingdom of God. Not for political gain, but for the defense of the vulnerable. Not for applause, but because Christ Himself commands it: "For I was a stranger and you welcomed Me" (Matthew 25:35).

America the way it is today may break our hearts. But America the way it could be—if it repents, if it turns, if it remembers—can still be restored.

Where sin abounds, grace can abound all the more. Where darkness spreads, light can still rise. Where justice falters, God can still work righteousness.

The question is whether the nation will listen. And whether the Church—the one institution entrusted with eternal truth—will find its voice before the hour grows too late.

Where Is the Church?

If America has lost her way, the greater tragedy is that the Church has lost her voice. The silence of believers in the face of suffering is not neutrality—it is complicity. The prophets of old would have called it what it is: fear of man disguised as prudence, comfort mistaken for holiness.

PART III

   Where are the pastors who once spoke truth to kings? Where are the shepherds who defended the flock instead of aligning with power? Where are the watchmen on the wall—the very people who celebrate their religious freedom—now that strangers, sojourners, and brothers in Christ are being torn from their families just a few miles from their sanctuaries?
   Believers send missionaries across oceans but remain silent when the persecuted stand at their own doorstep. They sponsor prayer campaigns for Christians suffering in Nigeria, Iran, or China, yet look away when fellow believers are rounded up in American streets, shackled, and placed in modern detention camps for the "crime" of seeking refuge. They grieve the persecution of Christians abroad while ignoring those imprisoned in their own backyard.
   This is not the Gospel. It is moral cowardice baptized in patriotic sentiment. Scripture leaves no ambiguity on this point.
God commands His people:

> "Execute true justice, show mercy and compassion
>   everyone to his brother.
> Do not oppress the widow or the fatherless,
>   the alien or the poor."
> (Zechariah 7:9–10, NKJV)

   To welcome the immigrant is not merely an act of compassion—it is obedience. A nation that claims to honor Christian values cannot turn its back on those who embody the biblical stranger, the resident alien, the sojourner, and even the face of Christ Himself. To do so is not only a moral failure; it is a betrayal of the faith America professes to uphold.
   The Lord Jesus did not call His followers to seek safety; He commanded them to bear the cross. Freedom that is not used for righteousness becomes complicity in evil. And when believers choose silence over solidarity, comfort over courage, nationalism over neighbor-love, the witness of the Gospel becomes hollow—worship without cost, faith without works, sermons without integrity.

> "Rescue those who are being taken away to death;
>   hold back those who are stumbling to the slaughter.
> If you say, 'Behold, we did not know this,'
>   does not He who weighs the heart perceive it?"
> (Proverbs 24:11–12)

   The question is not whether God has spoken—He has. The real question, the one that will define the legacy of this generation, is whether His people will obey.
   And this is where my story begins.

My experience with American immigration and removal proceedings confronted me with two competing legacies: the America people believe in—the one held up before the world as a beacon of justice—and the America now being shaped beneath the surface, increasingly detached from biblical truth and moral clarity. One is built on faith, dignity, and freedom; the other on fear, suspicion, and lies.

The Church must decide which legacy it will defend.

If the body of Christ does not speak for the stranger, who will? If we do not defend the persecuted, what remains of our witness? If we do not stand with the oppressed, how can we claim to follow the One who was Himself carried as a refugee into a foreign land?

America does not need another debate. It needs a moral awakening.

It needs pulpits that thunder with truth. It needs believers who refuse to bow to fear. It needs churches willing to open their doors not just to the comfortable, but to the detained, the displaced, and the despised.

For the measure of a nation is not the power it wields but the mercy it shows.

And the measure of a Church is not the size of its congregation but the courage of its compassion.

A Call to Repentance and Renewal

If the heart of the nation has grown cold, then the silence of the Church is its frost. The judgment of God rarely begins in the streets—it begins in the sanctuary. Before Babylon captured Jerusalem, before Rome fell to ruin, before every empire lost its soul, the prophets warned the same thing: that God's people had traded obedience for comfort and holiness for reputation.

The Church in America stands at that same threshold. It has grown accustomed to ease, mistaking comfort for blessing and applause for anointing. It has built sanctuaries of glass and steel but forgotten the altar of repentance. It has defended political platforms with more zeal than it has defended truth. And it has blessed the sword of the state while neglecting the suffering of the stranger.

Yet the voice of the Lord still calls:

> "If My people who are called by My name humble themselves,
>   and pray and seek My face
> and turn from their wicked ways,
>   then I will hear from heaven
> and will forgive their sin
>   and heal their land."
> (2 Chronicles 7:14)

Repentance must begin not in Congress but in the congregation; not in the courts, but in the hearts of believers who remember that the Kingdom of God is not built on ballots, borders, or budgets—but on truth, mercy, and justice.

The Church cannot remain neutral in an age of moral collapse. To be silent in the face of evil is to consent to it. To avoid controversy while souls are crushed beneath the machinery of injustice is to deny the cross we claim to carry. Jesus did not die to make His followers comfortable—He died to make them holy.

If the Church does not awaken, America will not endure. Political reform cannot save what spiritual decay has already consumed. A nation's laws may restrain wrongdoing, but only righteousness can restore its soul. The hope of this nation lies not in the next election, but in the next revival—in pulpits reclaimed by truth, in believers who fear God more than they fear man, and in churches willing to stand where it costs them something to stand.

The time for selective obedience is over. The time for polished sermons and timid faith is past. What this hour demands is courage—the courage to speak truth in love, to confront sin without compromise, and to remember that the God who judged Babylon and Rome still reigns over the nations today.

"For it is time for judgment to begin at the household of God." (1 Peter 4:17)

If America is to be healed, the Church must first be broken. Only through repentance can she recover her power. Only through humility can she regain her authority. Only through truth can she reclaim her witness.

The question is no longer whether judgment is coming—it is whether the Church will stand as salt and light when it does.

www.ingramcontent.com/pod-product-compliance
Lightning Source LLC
Chambersburg PA
CBHW020554030426
42337CB00013B/1095